EXPANDING HISTORICAL CONSCIOUSNESS

EXPANDING HISTORICAL CONSCIOUSNESS

The Development of the
Holocaust Educational Foundation

Anita Weiner

HOLOCAUST EDUCATIONAL FOUNDATION   SKOKIE, ILLINOIS

Printed in the United States of America

ISBN 0-8101-1453-4 (cloth)
ISBN 0-8101-1773-8 (paper)

Library of Congress Cataloging-in-Publication Data
Weiner, Anita.
Expanding historical consciousness : the development of the Holocaust Educational Foundation /
Anita Weiner.
    p. cm.
Includes bibliographical references and index.
    ISBN 0-8101-1453-4 (cloth : alk. paper)—ISBN 0-8101-1773-8 (pbk. : alk. paper)
    1. Holocaust Educational Foundation—History. 2. Holocaust, Jewish (1939–1945)—Study and
teaching (Higher)—United States. 3. Weiss, Theodore Zev, 1931– 4. Holocaust survivors—
Illinois—Biography. 5. Educators—Illinois—Biography. I. Title.
D804.33 .W45 2003
940.53'18'071073—dc21

                                                                                      2002151798

The paper used in this publication meets the minimum requirements of the
American National Standard for Information Sciences—Permanence of Paper for
Printed Library Materials, ANSI Z39.48-1984

To Zev and his supporters, who despite much evidence of man's inhumanity to man continue to work tirelessly at the task of improving the world through education

DEDICATION

It is with love and great respect for my parents and the values they cherished that I dedicate this volume in loving memory of

Arthur David and Pearl Slavin Malkin

My parents, Arthur and Perle Malkin, were both fortunate in not having had members of their immediate families suffer the horror that engulfed Europe during the 1930s and World War II. I believe it appropriate that this volume be dedicated to them because I feel that the values that they instilled in my brothers and me—a strong belief in family, the inherent dignity of all men, and the need for genuine charity and education—are the best defense against the Holocaust happening again.

My parents participated in organized activities as a way of expressing these beliefs. My father was active in the Anti-Defamation League, and particularly active in causing Chicago department stores to stop discriminating in their hiring practices. My mother served as president of a cancer research fundraising board. The strongest expression of their values, however, was in their serious approach to everyday living. They did not simply preach a set of abstract beliefs. They practiced them, and expected our family to do the same.

Judd D. Malkin
The Holocaust Educational Foundation

Contents

Prologue

Learning remains the best antidote to humanity's most inhumane impulses.

Theodore Zev Weiss

ON SEPTEMBER 30, 1999, ABOUT A HUNDRED FRIENDS AND SUPPORTERS of Zev Weiss and the Holocaust Educational Foundation gathered at a formal dinner to celebrate the establishment of the Theodore Zev Weiss Holocaust Educational Foundation Chair in Holocaust Studies, which had been officially launched at Northwestern University. Through the establishment of this chair, Holocaust studies would be part of the Northwestern curriculum for as long as the university itself exists. It was a moment of intense pride for the small group, which had worked together for over twenty years, sharing with Zev Weiss, the Foundation's leader and inspirational guide, in the various struggles and achievements that had made this moment possible.

None of the dozen individuals who had been invited by Zev Weiss and his wife, Alice, to their home on a summer evening in 1976 had anticipated this. They were invited in order to discuss the launching of a Holocaust memorial project and could not then anticipate either the growing climate of interest in the Holocaust throughout the country or the many project developments that would be carried out within the next two decades. Beginning with the videotaping of Holocaust survivor testimonials, this small group of Foundation supporters moved into the introduction of Holocaust courses at over 300 institutions of higher education around the country. They support those courses through biennial international conferences, a yearly summer institute, the East European Study Seminar, and finally the establishment of several international institutions for the introduction of Holocaust education in the former Soviet Union and Western Europe.

The Foundation, which was established that summer evening in 1976, has been described as a small organization, run on a shoe-string, that has, in a relatively short time, had a major impact on its area of focus—Holocaust education. Virtually all of the funds expended by the Foundation are directed toward its expanding activities rather than toward public relations with its accompanying glossy brochures. Therefore, very little is known about the organization itself and its history, even to the many hundreds of academic scholars actively involved in Holocaust education through the Foundation's outreach. The story of this Foundation, the people who are involved in it, and the development of its activities forms the central focus of this writing.

How the Holocaust became an acknowledged part of Western consciousness has become a historical field of study in itself, generating a growing number of scholarly and not-so-scholarly books. The Holocaust is now recognized as a major historical event, although for several decades it was first obscured, ignored, and repressed, then hesitantly noticed, selectively distorted to serve the needs of the hour, and finally acknowledged, studied, used, abused, denied, politicized, trivialized, and sanctified. The role of the Foundation in this story, which is both an honorable and a significant one, has been largely unacknowledged. It is hoped that this work will rectify some portion of this imbalance.

A member of the Holocaust Educational Foundation Board of Directors decided that the time had come for this story to be told. His financial contribution specifically allocated for that purpose made it possible to begin the process of gathering the necessary information. Since the fall of 1999 most of the board members were interviewed, as well as forty-eight academics who were teaching Holocaust courses throughout the country from Oregon to Maine and from Mississippi to North Dakota. These academics included internationally recognized Holocaust scholars, as well as professors of history, sociology, theology, psychology, philosophy, and literature who were teaching courses on the Holocaust within their own fields of expertise. This also included graduate-student teaching assistants working on Holocaust-related dissertations. In addition, numerous documents, letters of application, student evaluations, and faculty reports were read, as well as books and articles on the development of Holocaust awareness throughout the Western world.

The cooperation of both board members and academics was warm, spontaneous, and genuine. Most of those interviewed were pleased to have an opportunity to tell about how they had become involved in Holocaust studies through their contacts with Zev Weiss and the Foundation, and there was virtually universal admiration for the quality of the Lessons and Legacies Conferences, the Institute on Holocaust and Jewish Civilization, and the East European Study Seminar. One of the major challenges in summarizing these interviews has been to describe the development of these projects without an overdose of the repeated superlatives.

The summary presented here is divided into four parts. Part I deals with the Foundation's early years. This includes a description of Theodore Zev Weiss, of the formation of the Board of Directors, and of its first major project: the videotaping of survivor testimonies. Part II, which forms the major portion of this writing, describes the development of the Foundation's outreach to North American universities, colleges, and military academies; the courses that were developed; the goals of these courses and their impact on students; and the ongoing development of Holocaust awareness in the country. Part III describes the accompanying projects and institutions created to support the academic outreach: the Lessons and Legacies Conferences, the Institute on Holocaust and Jewish Civilization, and the East European Study Seminar. Finally, Part IV outlines the newly created international projects and the visions of future activities and organizations.

P · A · R · T   I

Background

THE STORY OF THEODORE ZEV WEISS AND OF THE HOLOCAUST EDU-
cational Foundation Board has been intertwined from the first moment that Zev and his family moved from Akron, Ohio, to Wilmette,
Illinois, a suburb of Chicago, in 1971. According to Earl Abramson,
who has been chairman of the Foundation's Board of Directors since
its inception, he was the one who brought Zev to Chicago. At that
time Earl was chairman of the school board of the local Beth Hillel
Academy. The school, which had over five hundred children, was
seeking an educational director, and Earl contacted Zev, who was already known to and highly recommended by the synagogue's rabbi,
Robert Hammer. When Earl phoned Zev and invited him, Earl said,
"Do you want to spend the rest of your life in Akron? I'll show you
the big city. Come to Chicago."

Zev stayed with the Abramsons, liked what he saw, accepted the
position, and bought a modest home in Wilmette. He then continued to work as director of the local Beth Hillel Academy until his re-
tirement in 1993. He and his wife still live in the home on Big Tree
Lane that they bought in 1971.

Although the meeting in 1976 led to the creation of the Holocaust Educational Foundation, the idea of an educational project on
the Holocaust began many decades earlier as the dream of a fifteen-
year-old, and it is on this background that the achievements of the
Foundation have been built. Describing the ongoing goals, projects,
setbacks, and accomplishments of the Foundation is in and of itself a
dramatic, absorbing process, but beginning with the dreams of that
fifteen-year-old is essential.

Theodore Zev Weiss

ZEV WEISS, WHO IS OFTEN TOLD THAT HE IS A TALLER ELIE WIESEL look-alike, was born in Demecser, Hungary, in 1931. His family lived the life of a traditional Central European Jewish family from a small town. Their town was in a region that was claimed by an unending series of disputing rulers. The region had a short period of independence, but during the past century it had also been part of Hungary and the Austro-Hungarian empire. The impact of these changes on life in Demecser was mainly through the addition of another language to learn, and there was nothing during his early years that could prepare Zev, his family, or the other Jews in the town for the catastrophes that awaited them.

In April 1944, when Zev was twelve years old, all the Jews were concentrated in the local ghetto. In June, on the second day of the Shavuot spring festival, they were sent to Auschwitz-Birkenau. He survived that death camp and was sent to Glevitz, where he participated in the death march from Glevitz to Sachsenhausen. Subsequently, Zev was sent to Mauthausen and then to Gunskirchen, from which he was liberated by the American army on the last day of the war, May 8, 1945, when he was thirteen years old. He seldom speaks of that period of his life, but during the years that followed, he formed the resolve that one day the story of what happened to European Jewry would become known to the world.

After liberation, Zev returned to his hometown for one day only and left because he found that no relatives had survived and because the neighbors who had taken over their homes threatened to kill him. He found a group of young Jewish survivors through an office that had been set up by the American Jewish Joint Distribution Committee (JDC). These young people had been gathered together in preparation for aliyah (migration to Israel) by emissaries sent to Europe for this purpose from Israel, then called Palestine. The group was brought by the JDC to Salzburg, and then to Badgastein, Austria. Between January and March of 1946 the group trekked by foot and by truck to a boat in Italy, which brought them to the shores of Palestine.

From the deck of the boat they could see the Haifa port, but because of the British Mandate policy, which responded to Arab pressure and severely restricted Jewish immigration, the boat was not allowed to dock, and they were turned back. The group had to make the long trek back to Badgastein, where Zev remained and studied in the school created there until January 1947. He wanted to go to Israel again, but there were still no signs that this would be possible, and each week another member of their small group left for either the United States or Canada. When only a few members of his group were left, they were asked whether they would like to go to Canada. Although he had no idea what this could be like, he saw that one by one everyone had raised his or her hand, including a girl whom he had befriended. He realized that there was really no choice, so he raised his hand also. He was the last member of the group to do so, and he found himself on a boat to Canada in January 1947. When they arrived, they were sent to various locations, and Zev was sent with a small group of young Jewish orphans like himself to Hamilton, Ontario, where he spent three or four months.

He then faced a new and formidable series of hardships that are perhaps not generally well known to the North American public. The young Jewish orphans who arrived from Europe were not warmly received by the local communities. The Canadian Jewish Congress offered food, clothing, and a place to stay for the first few months. After that, these young refugees—who spoke no English and who had just survived some of the most traumatic experiences in human history—were expected to go out and find jobs on their own in order to support themselves. Since they came without school certificates and had been without recognized schooling for a number of years, they were generally expected to become manual laborers. However, Canada was still in the process of absorbing returned veterans of the Second World War, and there were few jobs available. Although Canada is not generally considered a country with problems of anti-Semitism, many of these homeless, young Jews, fluent in neither English nor French and without family or recognized education, were told by firms to which they applied that Jews were not hired.

Most of the young Jews who arrived with Zev absorbed the expectations of those around them and ultimately settled for whatever jobs they could find. They remained shippers, tailors, or other kinds of unskilled or semiskilled laborers for much of their lives. Zev, however, had other dreams, and there was one man in Hamilton who took an interest in him. Ken Soble, a warm-hearted, self-made Jewish businessman, owned one of Canada's largest television networks and was active in the local Jewish and general communities. He invited Zev to his home during those first weeks in Canada, gave him twenty dollars, and said to him, "You can make something of your life. Go to Montreal, where there is a larger Jewish community and more opportunities."

While still only fifteen years old, Zev purchased a train ticket to Montreal and arrived there one evening with $10 in his pocket and nowhere to go. He walked about five miles from the Canadian National Railway station to the Jewish library and spent his first night in Montreal sleeping there on the floor. When he started looking for work, he found that jobs were scarce, particularly for Jews. While formulating his dream, Zev had to face the ongoing problems of supporting himself in order to eat and have a place to live. At the same time, he also had to learn English, and he wanted to find some way to become educated. He took any night job available, from putting up pins in a bowling alley to working a shift in a bakery, and went often to study in the evenings with Rabbi Pinchas Hirschprung and three or four others at the Lubavitch yeshiva, where he could warm himself from the freezing Montreal winter. Rabbi Hirschprung, who had also recently arrived from Europe and was himself struggling to make ends meet, made sure that Zev would eat a good meal each time he came, helped him to find work, and offered him whatever aid he could even though he himself had little money of his own.

From his schooling at Badgastein, where he had studied with some fine teachers such as Zorach Kramer, Zev had an excellent background in mathematics, geography, and history because those were the areas in which his teachers excelled. On the other hand, there were also many gaps in his general knowledge. Before the war he had been fluent in Hungarian, Czech, and Yiddish and had learned a good deal of Hebrew. By the time the war ended, Zev had added two more languages, Polish and German, which he spoke fluently. Learning English was certainly a challenge that he could meet. He managed to attend some classes for newcomers at Baron Bing High School in Montreal, and whenever possible he studied English at Herzeliah Jewish High School with a teacher named Klein, who later became a poet laureate of Canada. Klein befriended Zev and did what he could to be of help. Because Zev had to work to support himself, he could attend classes only during the few hours when he was not working.

Driven by the need to make something of his life and to earn a degree, Zev applied to McGill University. Although he lacked the required formal certification and did not pass the English exam, Zev did sufficiently well on most of the Quebec college entrance examinations to be accepted by the university. However, he had no money for tuition, and with his letter of acceptance in hand he went to the Canadian Jewish Congress to seek financial aid. Because of his refugee status, the people he spoke to there were unwilling to help him and advised him either to work at a trade such as woodcutting or to take whatever job he could get for the money if he needed it. According to Zev, "Nobody wanted to have anything to do with you. They thought there was something wrong with you." In part because of this kind of discouragement, only a handful of those who came over when he did ultimately continued their education. Zev was one of them.

Zev discovered that the Hebrew Teachers Seminary in Montreal had a program to train teachers. Zev applied and after an interview with Dr. Rieger, the Dean of the Seminary, he was accepted where he could exchange credits with the School of Education at McGill, and he registered there as well. He was awarded a two-year scholarship. Student tuition had to be paid in advance, and Zev did not have the money. He made an appointment with McGill's dean of students and was able to arrange for delayed payment during the course of the year. It was not easy for him to take courses at both McGill and the Hebrew Teachers Seminary while earning enough money to pay for food, tuition, a place to live, and a way to keep soles on his shoes during the long Montreal winters. The monthly twenty-dollar stipend he received from the seminary was very helpful.

Although he was still not quite sure how he wanted to accomplish his long-term vision, Zev had already decided that he would become a Jewish educator in order to help rebuild what was lost. Carrying forward the broader vision that was developing within him did not become a burning issue for him until the 1960s. In the meantime, he seldom spoke about the year he had spent between his deportation to Auschwitz-Birkenau and his liberation because, according to Zev, "It was still sort of something that you don't talk about. It happened. It's in the world; it's in your life. You know, spring has come and you forget about the winter. I didn't quite forget because deep down that's what I wanted to do." In order to get some teaching experience, Zev commuted on Saturday nights to Sherbrooke, a small community in Quebec. To earn ten dollars a week, he took the midnight train, taught Sunday School, and then returned on the afternoon train to Montreal to attend classes on Monday.

When he graduated from the seminary, Zev immediately got a job teaching at the local Talmud Torah. He had become a Canadian citizen, and life slowly began to improve. In 1955 he saw an advertisement in the Hebrew newspaper *HaDoar* for an assistant principal of a synagogue school in Rochester, New York. Deciding he had nothing to lose, Zev applied for the job and was contacted by the principal, Dr. Jay Stern. When asked on the phone whether he thought he qualified for the job, Zev answered, "Listen, I think I'll be good. I don't have any administrative experience, but I think I can do it." He was invited to come for an interview and was sent a ticket since he did not have the money for the train journey. He and the principal hit it off, but he also had to be interviewed by the rabbi. Stern prepared him for the interview by saying, "Whatever he asks you, be nice to him and say yes, because he's leaving anyway." According to Zev, the interview went well until the rabbi asked him what magazines he read. Zev told him that he read *Bitaon*, a Canadian Jewish Teachers' Federation magazine. The rabbi said, "I never heard of it," so Zev said, "Maybe you should." Fortunately, the rabbi took this in a positive vein and asked Zev to send him a copy. Zev was offered the job and began to work in Rochester in the summer of 1956.

Zev taught in the school, which had twelve hundred students, and was also put in charge of the youth program, where he was given considerable leeway for creativity. He loved what he was doing, was good at it, and to a degree felt that he had at last begun to work at what would lead him closer to the vision he had been guarding for the past ten years. Soon after he had arrived in Rochester, Zev faced a serious difficulty. Although he was not an American citizen, he received a draft notification. In the aftermath of the Korean War, legal immigrants were automatically subject to the draft. Knowing Zev's personal history, the chairman of the board of the synagogue was concerned, but when Zev went to the draft board he received a deferment, which was never activated. This enabled Zev to gain two years of invaluable experience working with and learning from Dr. Stern, who was a master of Jewish education. Zev also applied for admission and was accepted to the School of Education at Harvard, where he began to take graduate courses.

Rochester was a wonderful place to begin a new life, and Zev became close friends with the congregation's new rabbi, Abraham Karp, and with his family. Rabbi Karp's parents had come to the United States shortly before the Second World War, and he was interested in Zev's past life, which for Zev was a new experience. Many Friday evenings were spent with the Karp family, and the relationship has continued through the years. Zev made sure that the Holocaust was remembered in Rochester, but it was still not a time when people in general were interested in hearing about what had taken place. Although he was both appreciated and loved there, and could have remained in Rochester for the rest of his career, Zev had dreams that he could not have fulfilled in the position of assistant principal.

Zev therefore took a job in 1958 as principal of a synagogue school in Schenectady, New York. There he met his future wife, Alice, who was an assistant professor at the State University of New York in Albany. They married in 1962 and continued to live in Schenectady for two more years. In a strange twist of fate, Zev was then invited to direct a large synagogue school in Hamilton, Ontario, where he had first arrived at the age of fifteen. During his years in Schenectady Zev had continued to take courses at Harvard Graduate School of Education. It was not feasible for him at the time to go to school full time, and he and Alice left for Canada. Ken Soble was still in Hamilton and warmly welcomed the young couple to his home. Deborah, their first child, was born during the three years they spent there. Daniel, their second child, was born in Akron, Ohio.

By the time they came to Akron in 1967, Zev was ready to begin to implement his dream. For a while he toyed with the idea of starting his own private school, and at one time he bought a piece of property near Poughkeepsie, New York, for which he went into debt. He began to discuss his ideas with people associated with universities in the Akron area, but they were not ready to consider the subject and advised Zev to "let bygones be bygones." The level of understanding was quite shallow, and Zev was only able to implement one project with Rabbi Robert Hammer, then rabbi at the Akron synagogue where Zev was working. They managed to put together a filmstrip on the Holocaust for general high schools and synagogue schools. Rabbi Hammer was the film narrator, and the pictures included were ones that Zev had collected over the years. He used his own money to mail out copies of the filmstrip to public and private high schools all over the country. The film got very good reviews.

When Zev and Alice moved to Wilmette, Illinois, in 1971, the force within him urging him to move ahead with his vision could no longer be suppressed. Earl Abramson had invited him to become director of the synagogue's large school, but it took a few years for the educational routine at the school to run smoothly enough for him to concentrate on how to begin his personal mission. The general climate in the country had finally changed, and it was now possible to talk about what had happened to European Jewry during the Hitler years. Everywhere they had lived, Zev and Alice had made close, devoted friends, and Wilmette was no exception. Before long, the parents who sent their children to the synagogue school began to realize that their school director was an unusual person with a deep, unswerving commitment to their children, to Jewish education, and to some larger vision as yet undefined. When Zev was finally ready to express his ideas, he had a small group of loyal, devoted friends who were prepared to listen and follow his lead.

Forming the Holocaust Educational
Foundation Board of Directors

ON A SUNDAY EVENING IN THE SUMMER OF 1976, ZEV, WHO WAS working full-time as educational director at Beth Hillel Academy in Wilmette, phoned a few of his friends and invited them to his home for a meeting. The group that gathered in Zev and Alice's living room included Earl Abramson, Chaya Roth, Gitta Fajerstein Walchirk, Howard Stone, Mort and Sabra Minkus, Bob Stempel, Leonard Berlin, Lawrence Gerber, and Raya Schapiro. Zev explained to these friends that for many years he had felt a debt to those who were no longer here to let the world know about the victims and perpetrators of the Holocaust and about how human beings can and did behave. Although the vast majority of European Jewry had been brutally killed during the Nazi conquests between 1939 and 1945, it is estimated that between 50,000 and 100,000 managed to survive the camps and the final death marches. By the late 1970s most of these people who were still alive were no longer young. Zev proposed that the group's first project should be to document the firsthand accounts of as many survivors as possible through videotaping their stories before it was no longer possible to do so. He explained to those gathered in his living room that without the availability of authentic, firsthand testimonials, it would not be possible to transmit information about what had happened to future generations. Zev was not aware of any other group doing this at the time, and it was still well before such videotaping was undertaken by Steven Spielberg's organization.

From Zev's perspective, the reaction to his presentation was basically positive, though somewhat skeptical. The feeling Zev got was basically, "If you want to do it, we'll help you, but we don't hold out too much hope that you are going to succeed." Howard Stone, who immediately became the group's treasurer, remembers feeling more enthusiastic. Details of logistics and infrastructure were not discussed at that time, but Stone thought it was a wonderful idea, and he also was not aware of anyone else doing this kind of recording. It was the first he had heard of such an activity. Chaya Roth, herself a hidden child during the war years, was also favorable. According to Sabra Minkus's recollections of this early period, however, Zev's feeling that the group had been skeptical was justified: "We all underestimated how effective Zev was."

That same evening, knowing Zev's background and his passion for beginning the project, Howard Stone approached Zev and suggested that they arrange a fund-raising meeting to buy the necessary tapes and technical equipment. Purchasing these items and hiring someone to operate the equipment would require money. In addition, the interviews were likely to be a difficult, perhaps even traumatic, experience for the survivors, and it would probably be necessary to arrange for a psychologist or a social worker to be present.

Zev, however, did not wait. The next day he ordered $3,000 of videotapes, taking a personal loan to cover expenses. Not every wife would have accepted this behavior with equanimity, but Alice could always be counted on to give her husband the support he needed. She knew that once his mind was made up to follow some portion of his overall vision, very little could stop him; and despite the personal risks, she took pride in his ongoing accomplishments.

Since both Chaya Roth and her sister, Gitta Fajerstein Walchirk, were professional therapists, Zev immediately asked them to set up a meeting for a team of professional interviewers. Chaya and Gitta put together a list of ten psychiatrists, psychologists, and social workers whom Zev called and invited to a meeting at his home. All those he called responded positively, and this was the group of individuals who became the organization's Professional Advisory Board and volunteer interviewing team.

In the meantime, Lawrence Gerber, an attorney, applied for a charter and began the long process of legally incorporating the organization. (The Holocaust Educational Foundation was officially registered in 1981, with Earl Abramson as its chairman.) From Earl's point of view, once Zev had explained what he wanted to accomplish and had set out his goals, it was the responsibility of the Board of

Directors to see to it that he had the funds to accomplish these goals. The next step that year was to arrange for a fund-raising affair. Earl persuaded Bob Stempel to invite about twenty of his business acquaintances to his home. Zev spoke about his vision of beginning to engage in a process of Holocaust education, and all who were present recognized the depth of his conviction. He indicated that he would like to raise some money for the expenses involved in documenting the stories of Holocaust survivors.

That evening, checks with sums from $200 to $1,000 were collected from those assembled. The total was approximately $10,000, which was a good but modest beginning. The next day, however, Zev received a phone call from Bob Stempel, the evening's host. He wanted to know whether Zev would be at home within the next hour because a special-delivery letter was due to arrive for him. Zev assured him that he would remain at home, and when the letter arrived, he found in it a check for $50,000 from one of Bob's friends who had attended the meeting. That was a significant sum of money with which to begin. All the money was turned over to Howard Stone, the treasurer and financial advisor, who agreed that the Foundation now had the necessary seed money to move ahead. The following day, the major donor, who has always preferred to remain anonymous, called Zev and told him, "Just go ahead and do whatever you want. Don't worry about money."

This open mandate served only to increase Zev's instinctive caution about expenditures. Although he was often urged to do so, Zev never took any salary for his efforts, even after he retired and worked full-time on the Foundation's projects. He took great care to avoid all unnecessary costs and worked from his home for the first seventeen years until a board member provided the use of an office with no overhead costs in a nearby mall. During the video testimonial project, the money was spent only on the required video equipment and on an hourly salary for the technicians who filmed the interview. Later, Zev's generosity in support of Holocaust studies in academia became well known among scholars in the field. But with regard to the Foundation's overhead, Zev continued to maintain his caution, often at the cost of his own personal time and energy.

Zev was always interested in education, and during this early period he also proposed a project to the Foundation that involved working with public high schools. The idea was to work on high school history textbooks and to create a traveling library and museum van, staffed by volunteers, that would go from one public high school to another in order to bring some knowledge of the Holocaust to high school students. For many years Zev had examined high school text-books in the regions where he was living and had discovered that on average only three to four lines were devoted to this major event in human history. He proposed to the group that had now been formed that they attempt to find some ways to rectify such a flagrant omission.

Although this was to become the only project raised in the group that failed to materialize, most remember the idea of "the traveling school van" with fondness. Zev discovered early on that the logistics of such an operation were not within reach and that breaking into the rigidly organized high school bureaucracy was too great an obstacle to overcome.

With regard to the video testimonial project, it was clear that in order to do a professional job, considerable time and organization would be needed to prepare the interviewers, locate survivors, and arrange for a suitable place to interview them that had both privacy and an inviting atmosphere. Before momentum began to gather, how-ever, the project encountered a major setback. From the beginning, Zev had been both the visionary leader and the main source of or-ganizational implementation. Therefore, in 1979, when Zev under-went triple bypass surgery following some serious heart problems, the project was put on hold for about two years. Miraculously, he main-tained the strength of his motivation and commitment, and when his body had recovered much of its former strength, Zev called the group together and was ready to move forward.

Ongoing Activities of the Holocaust Educational Foundation Board of Directors

ONE OF THE MOST DISTINCTIVE CHARACTERISTICS OF THE BOARD OF Directors since that first meeting in 1976 at Zev and Alice's home has been its determined lack of formality. There is a deep commitment to a loose, flexible structure based on ease of communication, friendship, loyalty to Zev and to one another, and dedication to the goals that have been agreed upon. With the exception of one member, Mort Minkus, who died in 1992, all those who gathered in the Weiss's home in 1976 are still members of the board, along with several equally devoted members who joined over the years, including Sabra Minkus, Judd Malkin, Paul Krouse, and Jon Mills. Board members are proud that no time is wasted on unnecessary meetings or formalities, and the group gathers only when significant new decisions need to be made. Less important decisions are made over the phone or through individual visits with Zev or among board members. The focus of the board is on the issues involved in Holocaust education. It shuns bureaucratic procedures and concentrates on fundraising and advising Zev on his new ideas as they develop.

According to Earl Abramson, chairman of the Board of Directors since the Foundation's inception, in order to get an insight into the Foundation's organization, one must get an insight into Zev himself and his way of functioning. Remaining unswerving in his dedication to the mission of spreading Holocaust education, Zev's method of operation in the development of all of the Foundation's projects has been the discovery of decent, dedicated, and skilled individuals who are then trusted to carry out the educational goals agreed upon in whatever way they feel is most suitable. These people, whether they are volunteer professionals who interview survivors, graduate students, university professors, or internationally renowned Holocaust scholars, are given the specific support and encouragement that they require to dedicate themselves with greater ease to the task at hand.

No formal or bureaucratic procedures have developed at any stage of the Foundation's process of decision making. Since all Board members are businesspeople or professionals with full schedules, they are pleased to allow Zev considerable autonomy and feel comfortable with the system that has been worked out. All major projects that have been discussed and undertaken have succeeded well beyond anyone's expectations, and the consensus seems to be, as Earl Abramson succinctly put it, "We are staring down the muzzle of success. Don't mess with it. I don't argue with success." Whenever Zev felt that the time had come for some new development, he would telephone the board members individually. If the idea appeared to require a broader discussion, the group would come together to hammer things out. It was only during the period of videotaping testimonials that the Professional Advisory Board met frequently and regularly. Board members remember no more than seven or eight full board meetings since then, although there were frequent updates and informal contacts.

Fund-raising has been the key responsibility of the board, and the major portion of these funds has been raised from within the same small circle of devoted supporters. Although all board members are strongly dedicated to the educational goals of the Foundation, most of their financial contributions are made because of Zev's inspirational leadership. During the early years, expenses were relatively low and were covered as needed from a small bank account. Expenses increased as Zev expanded his vision and its accompanying implementation, and it was necessary to raise larger sums of money and to create some reserves. According to treasurer and financial advisor Howard Stone, although there have been times when the financial resources were stretched thin, Zev has around him a nucleus of people "who believe in him as a person, who believe in what he is doing, who have the wherewithal to help him do it."

In the summer of 1993, Zev met with Wendy Abrams, the daughter of a board member, and with her help formed an Associate Board with younger members, including some of Zev's former pupils. The key functions of this board have been to help with fund-raising efforts, to raise community awareness of the Foundation, and to ensure a measure of continuity. Although all of them are busy raising young families, each year since the fall of 1994 they have organized a major fund-raising event that has brought in as much as $50,000 yearly. The first three affairs were held in the Ravinia outdoor concert area, with a tent and dinner in the park, and the next three were sold-out theater events with Holocaust-related themes. Between two hundred and three hundred people have been in attendance, and these affairs have helped make the Foundation's activities better known to the larger Chicago community. After each of these affairs new members have been attracted to join the Associate Board.

The group has also sponsored seminars, book and film reviews, and lecture series attended by up to seventy-five people, and a visit was organized to the United States Holocaust Memorial Museum in Washington, D.C. Both Professor Peter Hayes of Northwestern University and Professor Christopher Browning of the University of North Carolina, prominent Holocaust scholars who are the key figures in the Foundation's academic activities, have been guests of the Associate Board. A social brunch was organized in 1994 so that the senior Board of Directors members could meet with the new Associate Board members, but most of their work has been independent, and the amount of interaction between the two groups has been limited.

According to all of those board members who were interviewed, no major controversy has arisen during their years of working together. Although most have freely admitted to feelings of skepticism and even disbelief at the possibility of achieving the various goals that Zev set before them over the years, the main feeling that comes across when speaking to them is one of awe at the extent of Zev's achievements. "The joke is on us," they say. None of them expected to be faced with such a vast range of activities to support and encourage, but the feelings of pride they take in being able to provide the necessary financial and emotional support are quite palpable. When there are differences of opinion—as there were, for example, about whether it was wise to extend the educational activities into the former Soviet Union—these differences are aired, and in the end everyone "comes aboard." Zev's vision has consistently proven far more successful than anticipated.

Testimonial Videotaping: The First Project

FOR THE FIRST DECADE OF ITS ACTIVITIES, THE HOLOCAUST EDUCA-
tional Foundation was engaged in the careful recording of firsthand
testimonials from several hundred survivors living in the Chicago
area, many of whom had never had the opportunity to tell their entire stories before. It was one of the first organizations in the world
that worked in an organized, systematic way to get these firsthand
narratives recorded, organized, and stored in a recognized repository
to be used for future education. A Professional Advisory Board was
formed of psychiatrists, psychologists, and social workers who all vol-
unteered their time to carry out the interviews.

They met regularly in order to establish a framework of clear-cut
goals and procedures that would guide them as they moved ahead.
Their overall goals were to establish an oral record of the Holocaust
that would be based on firsthand experiences and would remain in
a central repository for the education of future generations; to give
voice to the stories both of those who had survived but had found no
listeners and of those who were killed and were unable to speak; to establish a link between those who had been there and those who had
been spared; and to form a commitment toward the task of transmit-
ting the past as well as sensitizing others to present inequities with
their potential for future crimes and injustices. The backgrounds of
the interviewers ranged from several who had lived through years of
persecution and hiding as children, to others who had escaped from
Europe prior to the war years, and finally to some who were sensitive
to the Holocaust experience without having had any direct contact
with it.

As the goals and procedures were being established, Chaya Roth,
a member of both the Professional Advisory Board and the Board of

Directors, went to visit various campuses with her daughter, who was applying to colleges. At Yale she discovered that the first major archive devoted exclusively to videotaped testimonies of the Holocaust was in the process of being established. She gave Zev the necessary information, and he was informed by Professor Dori Laub, one of the archival directors at Yale, that the archive was encouraging local communities to videotape survivors in their area. Yale was willing to provide the services of a professional advisor who would offer a workshop in Chicago on Holocaust testimonial interviewing. Then, when the tapes were completed, the archive would be able to classify and preserve these testimonies, making them available for appropriate educational purposes.

Both the Board of Directors and the Professional Advisory Board were interested in making the connection with the Yale archive. On November 15, 1982, Zev attended the official inauguration of the Fortunoff Video Archive for Holocaust Testimonies at Yale, and during the following spring Professors Dori Laub and Geoffrey Hartman, the archive's professional advisor, came to Chicago to lead two workshops on interviewing survivors. Members of the Professional Advisory Board participated. They included Gitta Fajerstein Walchirk, Chaya Roth, Elsa Roth, Raya Schapiro, Allen Siegel, Fay Katlin, Lenore Blum, Ira Glick, Sondra Fineberg Kraff, Lya Dym Rosenblum, Elizabeth Jacob, Marilyn Silin, Marilyn Tallman, Elaine Shepp, Gordon Maguire, David Terman, and Barbara Newman. Some from this early group eventually dropped out, but a core of volunteers remained throughout the ten years of taping.

Although all these volunteers were mental health professionals who were experienced interviewers, the interviewing of survivors was a particularly sensitive procedure. Many had told only bits and pieces of their stories before and had never found anyone willing to listen from beginning to end. The volunteers were offered advice on how to prepare the interviewees, how to ask questions, how to create the least threatening atmosphere in order to put the survivors at ease, how to handle the potential traumas that might arise, and how to conduct a follow-up interview a month later to handle any aftereffects. The group decided that two interviewers should be present, one mainly as observer and the other more actively involved in encouraging the narrative. Although there were some differences of opinion among the professionals about the suitability of two interviewers, most went along with this group decision. Yale University and the Fortunoff Video Archive for Holocaust Testimonies also supplied release forms for the survivors to sign. This would give the archive the right to make the tape available for future learning. All the procedures involved—from phone call, to support, to taping, to the postinterview contact—were then reviewed and discussed with great intensity at the Professional Advisory Board's monthly meetings in order to ensure maximum sensitivity to interviewee's needs.

Next came the interview process. The Foundation had to find a technician who had suitable camera equipment and could maintain an unobtrusive presence in the room. The room itself would have to be suitable for interviewing and afford privacy, the necessary technical conditions for the videotape technician, and a nonthreatening atmosphere. For the first few years the interviewing and taping sessions were conducted in the library of Beth Hillel Synagogue. Several classrooms in the building were available as hospitality areas before and after the interviews for the interviewees and their families or friends who accompanied them. The library, however, was not sufficiently private, and there were occasional interruptions. A search was begun for better facilities.

By 1988, when the tapings were in full swing, Zev had already established an ongoing relationship with Peter Hayes, professor of German history at Northwestern University. Professor Hayes, who became the first academic consultant for the Foundation, helped find a more suitable location. He made a connection between Zev and Professor Michael Janeway, then Dean of the Northwestern School of Journalism, which had recently opened a new media facility. Zev was then able to negotiate arrangements for a shift to the new facilities and for the use of a camera and cameraman willing to work on Sundays and evenings. Although these new recording facilities were better and there were no interruptions, the general atmosphere was less congenial. With the change, something was gained, and something lost.

An announcement in the local Jewish paper, combined with a series of informal calls, brought the recording project to the attention of the Jewish community in nearby Skokie, where a number of survivors were living. The interviewers began with a nucleus of about twenty names. Relying mainly on word of mouth, the interviewers began to build up their contacts. Gradually, the number of people who were willing to be interviewed increased to a steady flow. There were very few refusals, and most of those who initially refused were ultimately persuaded to participate. Gitta Fajerstein Walchirk, an experienced social worker and a member of the original board, took charge of the complex interviewing procedure. She herself had been a hidden child during the war years, and since the Yale advisors had suggested that a Holocaust survivor should make the initial contact, it was Gitta Fajerstein Walchirk who made all of these initial phone calls.

During this first phone contact, which generally took half an hour, sufficient information was collected for a decision to be made as to how difficult the interview would be. Gitta carefully explained the procedure so that the survivors would be prepared, and an appointment was made for the interview. According to the agreed upon schedules, she chose the available professional and sent them relevant information prior to the appointment. The volunteer professional who would be conducting the interview called the survivor back within ten days of the initial phone call to introduce him- or herself and to ease any tension in the interviewee's mind. Arrangements were made for transportation when necessary, and a host or hostess was there to greet the survivor and make him or her comfortable before the interview began. Then, when the interview was completed, some form of closure was initiated, coffee was served, and an atmosphere of relaxation was created in the transition prior to the journey home. A follow-up contact was made several weeks later to bring some closure to the experience. This entire operation was run with a minimal budget and no overhead at all. The only one who was paid was the video technician. Most of those involved gave up one Sunday every four to six weeks when three or four interviews were conducted, each lasting a maximum of ninety minutes.

During the interview, people were encouraged to tell their stories chronologically, beginning with how the Holocaust first began in their lives, tracing through their experiences during the war years and the events surrounding their liberation, and ending with something of their present life and family situation. The emotional tone of those interviewed varied greatly, from highly emotional to matter-of-fact, and the experiences related also varied from ghettos, deportation, and death camps to hiding in forests and survival skills. The common themes when they began their stories were the gradual changes in their daily lives as the persecution increased—the growing restrictions, overcrowding and deprivations, the efforts to maintain a normal life under conditions of growing isolation and need, and the almost universal disbelief that what was happening could not be reversed. Those who experienced the camps focused mainly on the hunger, cold, fear, exhaustion, lice, and disease, as well as the shame and humiliations suffered. All had suffered losses and separations from family and emphasized the supreme importance of maintaining ties, which was essential to keeping up their motivation to survive.

During the summer of 1989 Gitta telephoned several dozen of those who had been interviewed in order to find out what impact the interview had had on them. Almost all remembered it as a positive experience, sometimes providing an opportunity to recognize inner feelings and memories that had been repressed. The opportunity to tell their story from beginning to end without interruption was particularly appreciated, and they were grateful that their experiences would become part of a permanent record of the Holocaust. Three of those interviewed later decided to make the journey back to their hometown and to the camps where they had been interred. The care that had gone into the process had, by and large, succeeded in preventing much of the traumatic impact that was feared and anticipated.

At the 1989 Lessons and Legacies Conference, which is described in Part III, the group of professionals who had planned and carried out the interviews made a presentation describing the testimonial project and summarized their activities for a chapter in the 1991 *Lessons and Legacies* volume. Over the years nearly three hundred testimonials were recorded, and the tapes were turned over to the Fortunoff Video Archive for Holocaust Testimonies. By this time, as shall be seen, an ongoing relationship had been established with Northwestern University, and copies of the tapes were given to the Northwestern University Library as well. When the Spielberg Foundation began its major survivor-interviewing campaign around 1995, most of the survivors in the Chicago area had already been interviewed through this pioneering Holocaust Educational Foundation project.

By then, the Holocaust Educational Foundation was launched on a much larger mission that involved all the board members and many members of the Professional Advisory Board as well. During this period the regular meetings of the Professional Advisory Board became less frequent, and by 1995 members were no longer meeting, although they continued to see one another informally and never officially disbanded. It was, however, this small group of dedicated mental health professionals that had made the Foundation's first major project, the videotaping of Holocaust testimonials, a successful one.

P · A · R · T   I · I

Expanding into New Educational Activities

AS THE VIDEOTAPING OF TESTIMONIALS PROGRESSED, ZEV BECAME IMpatient to begin implementing that portion of his vision closest to his heart: teaching the Holocaust so that young people would be able to learn the facts of what had occurred. With no political agenda and no specific perspective to advocate, Zev was deeply convinced that "learning remains the best antidote to humanity's most inhumane impulses."

He was still working full-time as educational director at Beth Hillel Academy, but the school was running smoothly and the staff was aware of Zev's passion to fulfill his vision. For a while Zev debated the merits of introducing Holocaust studies at the level of secondary schools or at the college level. He discovered how difficult it was to break into the rigid high school curriculum, and with the encouragement of the Board of Directors, Zev began to explore the possibility of actively introducing Holocaust studies into higher education. It was then the mid-1980s, and the Holocaust, which had been largely unrecognized as a major historical event, was becoming an acceptable topic for academic scholarship in perhaps a dozen institutions of higher learning throughout the country.

Zev's decision to work on breaking into the curriculum of higher education rather than secondary schools was a crucial turning point that has shaped the Holocaust Educational Foundation ever since. It was a unique decision that finds no parallel in other organizations or institutions dedicated to Holocaust memorialization. With this decision, Zev, supported by his board members, was the first and only one to set out on the path of changing American consciousness by changing higher education.

It took a while before Zev found what he was looking for. He began by contacting the history departments of various prestigious universities and inquired whether they would be willing to introduce a course on the Holocaust in their regular course offerings. The response was evasion, postponement, and general disinterest unless money was being offered for the establishment of a chair. Fortunately, Zev was still unaware of the procedural obstacles involved in introducing new courses at most universities, and he continued to pursue his goal with determination. When asked later whether he became discouraged at that time, he replied characteristically, "I never get discouraged."

NORTHWESTERN UNIVERSITY, NOTRE DAME, AND BEYOND

Zev's efforts were finally crowned with success in 1987. He contacted Northwestern University and requested the name of the professor in the history department who taught German history. Northwestern, from which many of the Foundation's board members had graduated, once had a quota on the admission of Jewish students, and a well-known Holocaust denier, Professor Arthur Butz, was still a faculty member in the university's engineering department. Zev was given the name of Professor Peter Hayes, and he made inquiries into Hayes's academic background and his status among the students and the faculty. The information he received was extremely positive. A German historian with an Irish Catholic background, Hayes had graduated magna cum laude from Bowdoin and then received a master's degree from Oxford University and a doctorate from Yale. He was known as one of the most popular lecturers on campus.

Hayes, an attractive, articulate, and engaging lecturer, was a well-respected historian of Nazi Germany and its international politics and interested in issues of morality, politics, human rights, and the abuse of power. His doctoral dissertation, later a prizewinning book, had investigated I. G. Farben, the German industrial firm that had built a factory outside Auschwitz using slave labor during the Second World War. One of his discoveries was that about 80 percent of the slave laborers who worked on that site either died there or were sent back to Auschwitz to be gassed. He taught courses on Germany during the Weimar and Nazi periods and had included some lectures on events related to the Holocaust. He had not, however, ever taught a course focused specifically on the Holocaust. When he worked on his original research, the Holocaust had not been considered a subject for historical inquiry in its own right. None of the early pioneers who began to teach the topic had taken a Holocaust course themselves when they were students because such courses were not available.

Early in 1987 Hayes received a phone call from Zev requesting a meeting. When they met at Hayes's university office, Zev came straight to the point and asked whether he would be willing to teach a course on the Holocaust. Zev remembers that Peter was interested and willing to listen, and Hayes himself remembers that he said "Sure." At that first meeting a partnership between the two was formed which became the basis of a major academic enterprise that proceeded to expand exponentially during the next decade.

The first obstacle to overcome was the large ongoing repertoire of courses Hayes had already obligated himself to teach. How could he fit in such a course? Zev asked him what would make it possible to do so and was told that if Zev could offer the history department enough "release time" money to hire someone who could teach Hayes's freshman seminar, then he would be able to teach a Holocaust course. Zev immediately produced the three thousand dollars required, and the Northwestern University history department granted approval for offering the course the next fall. In addition, during the summer of 1988 the Foundation sent Hayes to the Yad Vashem Holocaust Memorial Center in Jerusalem. Hayes, who was not sure how the students would receive a Holocaust course, agreed to try it out for a year and then decide whether to continue with it.

To the delight of Zev and the Board of Directors, Hayes offered his course on the Holocaust for the first time in the fall of 1988. Although it was not the first such course to be taught in the United States, it was the first taught through the outreach and encouragement of Zev and the Holocaust Educational Foundation. Much was made of the event in the local university newspaper, and fifty students registered—a higher number than was expected. The course was a great success, and the following year it had a registration of 150 students. The university's provost and president were pleased. Since 1988 the Northwestern course on the Holocaust has continued, and demand for places in the course has always exceeded the enrollment limit of 150.

With more confidence, in the spring of 1989 Zev called the

history department at the University of Notre Dame, perhaps America's best-known Catholic institution of higher education. He was given the name of Professor Robert Wegs as the expert in European history, and Zev called to make an appointment. Wegs found the call somewhat disconcerting, since he had no idea who Theodore Z. Weiss could be and was concerned that it might be someone with a negative agenda. He walked down the hall to the office of Professor Roger Brooks, a colleague who was teaching Jewish studies in Notre Dame's department of theology, and said to him, "Roger, I think we have a problem. I think I just agreed to have lunch with a Holocaust denier. There's a guy named Theodore Weiss from some Holocaust foundation, and you know what that might mean." Brooks agreed that it was suspicious, and Wegs suggested that he come along to the luncheon—"So if he starts steering things in that direction, we can cut him short and basically remove him from campus." Brooks concurred and commented, "But the first words out of this guy's mouth better be right, or we're standing up and walking out. Are we agreed?"

According to Brooks, he went to the luncheon and could see immediately that this man was not a Holocaust denier. Wegs, however, remained suspicious for the first half-hour that it took Zev to come around to his point. When he finally did mention that he was interested in having a course on the Holocaust taught at Notre Dame, Wegs was concerned, as most academics are when they feel that someone might attempt to limit their academic freedom. Zev then asked, "How can I help you two?" and Brooks said that if they were to consider teaching such a course they would need some support. When asked what kind of support, Brooks responded that in order to prepare a course, they would need to spend a month together in Yad Vashem to prepare for it. Zev immediately said "Done," and it was only then that Wegs realized Zev was serious. He was not telling them what to teach. He wanted them to make use of the study opportunities at Yad Vashem, and he was offering to pay for their trip.

Zev asked when they wanted to go. He then worked with his travel agent, set up a place for the two of them to stay in Jerusalem, and left the itinerary of their time there up to them. They could find a way to connect with Yad Vashem, work at a library, or do whatever they needed in order to set up their course. Wegs, a Catholic and a professor of Central European history, knew nothing about the Jewish civilization that had been lost in the Holocaust, while Brooks, a professor of Jewish studies, knew only the broadest historical events during that era. They decided to team-teach the course and made plans to travel together that summer. When all the arrangements had been made, less than a month prior to their departure, Brooks spoke to Zev and mentioned that they were probably missing a rare opportunity. If they could stop in Warsaw and visit Auschwitz on their way back from Israel, then their course would have greater authenticity. Zev agreed that it was a good idea and called back two hours later having made all the necessary arrangements.

Wegs and Brooks spent the month in Jerusalem working on course preparations, returned via Poland, and in the spring of 1990 offered a course titled "The Holocaust: Historical and Theological Perspectives." Both men had put their requests through the normal course approval procedures, including their own faculties in the history and theology departments, their area coordinators and, finally, the undergraduate coordinator. No one in the administration had raised an eyebrow; no obstacles were put in their path; and the room in which they taught, holding ninety students, was full. Zev visited that first class and made a presentation, and he has continued in this tradition throughout the years.

The members of the Board of Directors felt that Zev would be satisfied with five or six universities teaching courses on the Holocaust through the encouragement and support of the Foundation. With two university courses now launched, they felt that their mission was nearing completion. Zev, however, was only beginning, and one of his key supporters on the board was deeply impressed with the leverage potential that these courses afforded. He explained that his whole business was based on using leverage in the construction of buildings and that he had never found a situation with better leverage than providing an initial grant for setting up a course and then having the university carry on from there. Although he was still unaware of how many universities Zev would ultimately reach, he and the other members of the board were willing to continue their support without setting limits.

Zev went ahead with his calls and visits to other universities, and he was now helped through the use of Hayes's academic network of German historians. Hayes also recommended that he contact Professor Christopher Browning, who was then attending a Holocaust meeting in Oxford, England. Browning, who had begun his graduate studies in French history, became involved in Holocaust scholarship through a series of unanticipated life circumstances. In his first university teaching job, at Allegheny College, Pennsylvania, Browning was asked to teach a course on German history that was listed in the catalog. His course preparations led him first to Hannah Arendt and her intriguing concept of the banality of evil, and then, through her constant references, to Raul Hilberg's massive, thoroughly researched, and definitive monograph *The Destruction of the European Jews.*

Browning took more than a month to read this book, which literally changed the course of his life. He spent the years 1971 to 1974 completing a doctoral dissertation on the liaison between the Nazi foreign office and the satellite governments with regard to the deportations of Jews. He thereby became the first non-Jewish Holocaust expert in the academic world. This unique status resulted in many speaking engagements among Jewish groups. Through Professor George Mosse, who had been on his dissertation committee, he was afforded immediate and helpful access to many important Jewish scholars in the field. Browning accepted a position at Pacific Lutheran University in 1974. There he immediately introduced a course on the Holocaust and continued the research and publication that gradually made him one of the most respected scholars in the field.

Zev and Browning's first meeting was in a smoky English pub. Zev had been told to look for a tall fellow with a glass of wine in his hand, and that is how he found Browning, whose first impression of Zev was of an Elie Wiesel look-alike, only about six inches taller. Zev brought regards from Hayes, a friend and colleague of Browning's, and at their brief meeting Browning agreed to come to Northwestern sometime the following year to give a presentation. At the time, he doubted that he would hear from Zev again. Not long after, however, when doing research in Jerusalem, he got a letter from Hayes inviting him to a conference sponsored by the Holocaust Educational Foundation that would be held at Northwestern in the fall of 1989. In addition, even before the conference took place, Browning was asked to become an active academic consultant for the Foundation. He agreed to do so and began working with Zev and Hayes. Their concerns included recruiting Holocaust teachers and fund-raising.

Hayes and Browning were not only well known and respected scholars in the field but also congenial men who were genuinely interested in the development of Holocaust studies and in being of help to those who were new to the field. By involving these two professors in his projects, Zev was creating a crucial partnership. Hayes and Browning offered the imprimatur of their scholarship as well as a level of camaraderie and support that was universally acknowledged by all those who were later involved. Although Zev continued to do almost all the outreach, he depended on the professional advice and support of these two men through the years. As the number of projects expanded and the circle of academics who became actively involved grew, the atmosphere of both warm encouragement and serious scholarship was steadfastly maintained at the conferences, the summer institute, and the study tour.

ONGOING ACADEMIC OUTREACH

Zev's growing network of academic support was extremely helpful. Now when he called a university, he generally had the name of a professor he was interested in meeting, and he was already acquainted with that professor's scholarly interests. He found considerable willingness on the part of these professors to discuss the possibility of offering a course on the Holocaust, and the number of cooperating universities began to climb dramatically. With the backing of the Foundation, Zev offered each professor the specific help he or she required to introduce the course. That help might consist of paying the university for the teacher's required release time for preparation or purchasing a suitable library for the students and the professor. Professors frequently suggested the names of other colleagues who might be interested in teaching about the Holocaust.

The German Studies Association helped to give the Foundation some important exposure at that early period. During the summer of 1989, at the recommendation of Hayes, Professor Jay Baird (of Miami University in Ohio and then president of the Association) and Professor Gerald Kleinfeld (of the University of Arizona and the Association's executive director) invited Zev to hold a reception while the Association was having its annual convention in Bethesda, Maryland. Members of the Foundation's Professional Advisory Board, including Gitta Fajerstein Walchirk and Chaya Roth, worked hard to arrange for an attractive reception with good food that would be far more substantial than the usual wine and cheese served at such events. Much to their surprise, over a hundred of the convention participants came to the reception. Both Zev and Browning gave talks at the reception describing the goals of the Foundation, and many of the German historians who attended came up to Zev afterward and expressed an interest in teaching a course on the Holocaust. Zev made careful note of their names and phone numbers, and he consulted with Hayes and Browning about each of them. When he telephoned them, he felt more confident of success than when he had made his earlier attempts.

With the help of Hayes and Browning and the cooperation of the professors who had expressed interest at the German Studies Association meeting, by 1992 sixty-five colleges and universities had courses on the Holocaust that had been introduced with the help of the Foundation. Zev had visited most of them. As Michael Marrus, one of the first scholars to document the growth of the Holocaust as a field of study, has pointed out, during this period the Holocaust was being carefully studied by more and more historians. Their research findings and their scholarly publications were slowly adding to the historical understanding of a deeply traumatic period of world history. Only through such careful research and documentation could the manipulation of the mass media be countered by the weight of historical evidence. Most of those who were beginning to teach courses on the Holocaust through contact with the Holocaust Educational Foundation were scholars in German or European history whose contributions to research had not generally been in Holocaust studies. However, they began to contribute to the research both directly and indirectly. As each new course was added, the market for Holocaust research expanded, and more professors and their students bought books on the subject. Thus the Foundation was making a significant contribution to the growth of Holocaust research by providing the field with a steadily expanding market of interested readers.

The number of courses increased to one hundred during 1993, and it continued to climb with wholly unanticipated speed so that by the end of the century—only twelve years after Hayes at Northwestern became the first pioneer—there were nearly four hundred universities with which Zev and the Holocaust Educational Foundation had an ongoing relationship. Most of them had introduced courses on the Holocaust because of their contact with the Foundation. The geographical dispersion and the kinds of institutions involved varied widely. In nearly every state of the United States and in many Canadian provinces there are college courses being offered on the Holocaust thanks to Zev and the Holocaust Educational Foundation. The size of these host institutions also varies greatly, from large state universities such as Texas A&M, with close to 35,000 students, to small private colleges such as Agnes Scott, with less than eight hundred.

The academics who teach these courses are generally tenured faculty members who are mainly historians, particularly German historians, but there are also those who are members of sociology, literature, philosophy, psychology, Jewish studies, religion, theology, and political science departments. The large majority of these academics are not Jewish, and neither are the students they teach. The students come from small rural communities in the Midwest and the South, as well as from large metropolitan areas throughout North America. There are, however, some Jewish academics drawn to Holocaust studies because they were the children of Holocaust survivors or of parents who had fled Europe during the period of systematic persecution before the outbreak of war. Several of these Jewish academics, such as Nathan Cogan, professor of English literature at Portland State University in Oregon, have documented their family's experience as part of their teaching. The perspectives that both professors and students bring to their courses, according to the interviews described later, are varied. What professors do have in common is an interest in taking a major historical event that occurred in a Western society within the memory of the parents and grandparents of their students and analyzing this event in such a way that their students will begin to comprehend its significance and its relevance to their own lives.

Many of those interviewed had included some aspects of the Holocaust in their earlier course lectures but did not feel themselves sufficiently knowledgeable on the subject to offer a course exclusively on this subject. Some had actually considered doing so but lacked either the time required to organize such a course or available guidance on the best materials to use. Often an unanticipated phone call from Zev Weiss that seemed to come from out of the blue was their first contact with the Foundation.

Fairly typical was the response of Daniel Rogers, professor of European history at the University of Alabama in Mobile: "I don't think I actually was involved [in Holocaust studies] before the Foundation contacted me. I had studied German history and I had learned cer-

tainly about Nazi Germany and the Holocaust during my graduate
studies. But my research has always been in a later period, and it was
Zev Weiss calling and asking me to come to a conference that got me
involved for the first time in an in-depth way. Zev called me out of
the blue. I didn't know what he wanted. I have heard since from other
people that he did the same for them, too. It sort of almost sounded
as though you were being interrogated by somebody you didn't even
know. He called and asked, 'Do you teach about the Holocaust? And
why not?' A series of questions. And ultimately, once he satisfied himself that I was okay by talking to me in this fashion, he invited me to
the conference at the Foundation's expense.

"I think he was basically giving me an interview and I didn't realize it. I wasn't ready for it, didn't know it was coming. So, you know,
it's easy, in this situation, to wonder, 'Who is this person calling me?'
He's done that with a lot of people. It's fairly routine that he does that
kind of thing. So I went to the conference and found it to be absorbing and fascinating, and that there were many aspects of teaching European history that really would benefit from my knowing more
about the Holocaust. He offered in person, when I was there, to help
with the library. Whatever we needed to get a course going here.
And I proposed a course and launched it about a year after that first
conference."

If the conference was too far off, Zev would generally follow up
on his phone call with a visit to the university. Sometimes the first
person he contacted was the dean or the head of a department. This
was the procedure described by Professor Kathleen Dugan at the University of San Diego in California. "Mr. Weiss himself had come on
one of his journeys around the country, and had spoken to our dean,
who heard what the Foundation was doing and immediately trans-
ferred it to me. I was then the chair of the religious studies department, but he knew I was very interested in Jewish-Christian dialogue.
I am a theologian. I teach in the religious studies department and I
have been extremely interested in the Holocaust as a subject. So I began to prepare, under Mr. Weiss's urging, a course on the Holocaust
which had not been taught in our department. In fact, there had not
been a course taught in the university."

One of the incentives that made a significant difference was that
the support and encouragement of the Foundation was offered with

no strings attached. Unless the money was needed to pay the university for release time, once an academic had been approached, he or she was trusted to use whatever sums were offered according to his or her own academic judgment. According to Steven Hochstadt, a professor of German history at Bates College in Maine, "This was the moment when I was thinking about it and he arrived with encouragement and an offer of, I think, three thousand dollars to do whatever I wanted with, essentially. The money had no strings attached. In fact, at the time, the money meant nothing to me at all. I couldn't do anything with three thousand dollars, and I didn't need three thousand dollars. Much more interesting, and much more encouraging, was the fact that there was this man who was saying, 'I want you to teach about the Holocaust. I represent a group, and this is what we are doing. We think it's important.' This was right at the same time I was thinking maybe I want to do this. I was pondering about it." In fact, Hochstadt then used the money for a trip to Yad Vashem in Jerusalem, which became an important part of the preparation for a course that has consistently had the largest attendance of any course in Bates College over the past eight years.

Not all those interviewed were easily convinced that they should begin to offer a course on the Holocaust. Marvin Swartz, a professor of European history at the University of Massachusetts in Amherst, at first told Zev that he was not willing to do so. Swartz claimed that Zev "wouldn't let me go and I finally said yes, I would." When asked why he had been so reluctant, he explained, "The Holocaust is a very difficult subject to teach. It's emotionally draining, there are a lot of emotions stirred up by teaching it both in me and in the students, and I had never taught it before. I was not prepared to teach it, and I would have preferred not to at the time. To persuade me further, Zev agreed to give me some money to purchase books, as the Holocaust field was something that was not in my educational agenda. It wasn't available as a subject of study many years ago. And he provided assistance to the department to teach one of my courses so I would have time to bone up on Holocaust studies." The course that Swartz subsequently developed, despite his initial reluctance, has since elicited some student comments that are "usually highly favorable. Some say it's one of the best courses they've ever taken." This was a comment frequently repeated by those interviewed. The impact of these courses on the students are discussed at greater length later, but the tendency of student comments to be positive was virtually universal.

Only six or seven years after his first successful outreach to Hayes, it was no longer necessary for Zev always to initiate contact with universities. Those interested in teaching Holocaust courses have been reaching Zev and the Foundation on their own through referrals from colleagues who were involved, through Zev's early presentations at several of the German Studies Association's annual meetings, and more recently through a Web site organized by Professor David Meier from the University of North Dakota. Meier himself is an example of those who initiated such contact:

"The Foundation was having a special meeting at the German Studies Association meeting, I think it was in D.C., and I literally went in because I was curious about what they were doing. I talked with Zev Weiss, and I told him that in my opinion I had not developed the credentials of a Holocaust scholar, but as a modern German historian it was something that was important to me. It was a subject that I would very much like to know, and [I asked] if there were resources available that would assist me in offering a course on the Holocaust. At the same meeting, I talked with Christopher Browning and a number of others who were intimately associated with the Foundation, and I got a better feeling for it. Then a couple of weeks after the conference I received calls from the Foundation, and they very generously offered to assist me in obtaining exposure to the camps in Europe through a study tour that they were putting together."

Doris Bergen, a professor of history in Notre Dame's department of religion, had previously taught at the University of Vermont. She is another example of those who initiated contact with the Foundation, although she was already teaching a Holocaust course. "I can't remember the exact dates, but when I came to the University of Vermont, we had a community of people connected with the university who were starting a Holocaust studies program on the campus. One of the plans that we came up with was to teach a summer course for schoolteachers in the area, teachers who were teaching courses or units to seventh, eighth, or ninth grade level on the Holocaust and who wanted some extra training from scholars in the field. So we tried to set up a kind of interdisciplinary thing, where we had a historian, and an expert on anti-Semitism, and a religion professor. Then, when

I was trying to get together the funding for this course, someone told me, 'Call Zev Weiss.' I didn't know Zev Weiss at that point, but I got his number from somebody else in the field. It may have been from Peter Hayes. I called him in his place in Chicago, and he was extremely interested in what we were doing, extremely helpful. He arranged to meet with me at a conference that we were both going to be at, a German studies conference. So that's how I first met him and found out about the work of the Foundation. But it was one of those things that once I made the first call and found out about it, it seemed like everyone I talked to had some connection with the Holocaust Educational Foundation."

By the mid-1990s contact with the Foundation had become an accepted channel for academics interested in Holocaust studies. Lieutenant Colonel Lorrie Fenner, who taught the course at the U.S. Air Force Academy in Colorado, summed up the urgency of this contact succinctly. "I met him telephonically about a year before we did the course, because I told my department head that if I was going to do it, I wanted to do it right. And therefore that calls for some intense preparation on my part." Zev Weiss and the Holocaust Educational Foundation had become the recognized source of support for those who were interested in teaching about the Holocaust in institutions of higher education. Before Zev began his outreach to university campuses, there had been only a few academics, some of them well known, who had been teaching Holocaust courses on university campuses in North America. However, once Zev, with the backing of his Board of Directors, launched his initiative, the number of these courses increased dramatically. When Zev was ready to move, the field was ready to receive him. As we shall see, the time was ripe.

INTRODUCING HOLOCAUST STUDIES
IN THE MILITARY ACADEMIES

It is quite possible that the most significant contribution made by the Holocaust Educational Foundation to date has been through Zev's outreach to the three U.S. military academies. According to Brigadier General Carl Reddel, who made the decision, after meeting with Zev, to introduce the course into the curriculum of the Air Force Academy, the course has been a good one for the Academy in ways that he did not anticipate. He feels that as a result of his contact with Zev, a course has been introduced that is able to deal with issues of genocide in a professional manner. These are issues that have a strong relevance to the security of the United States, and they are highly relevant to a program of study for Air Force cadets. What was largely unanticipated was that the course not only has been a catalyst for profound reflection on the part of the cadets but also has had an impact on the entire Academy's community of thought and education through its effect on the military officers involved in teaching it. Unlike at the other military academies, the large majority of faculty members at the Air Force Academy are commissioned officers. As a result of their involvement in the preparation for and presentation of the Holocaust course, these officers have been exposed to many other disciplines and to a broader way of contemplating the issues related to genocide.

From Reddel's perspective, what has emerged through a combination of careful Holocaust course preparation and the relevance of contemporary world events is that the Air Force Academy has become involved in developing a new type of public servant. Perhaps the most challenging profession of the twentieth century in terms of intellectual demands and ethical dilemmas has been that of the military. Education must prepare a military officer of the twenty-first century to face ethnic conflicts and make decisions that affect civilian populations. The contribution of the Holocaust Educational Foundation has helped to introduce both faculty and students at the military academies to a course that analyzes the role of the military in mass murder with its ethical and legal, as well as military, implications and responsibilities.

As an officer and an academic, Reddel specialized in Russian studies and became aware, during his graduate studies, of how military decisions can, at times, have a major impact on people without sufficient regard for their needs. He had explored the issue of how the U.S. military dealt with Russian soldiers who did not want to return to Russia at the end of the Second World War. Although these men would cut their wrists and otherwise attempt to commit suicide, they were forced to go back. We now know that Stalin deliberately killed most of them when they returned. These studies had sensitized Reddel to the issues of military responsibility for ethical decisions in a changing world, and in his role as head of the history department in a military academy he sought opportunities to address this issue. The introduction of the Holocaust course gave him a clear-cut opportunity to confront the issue of military decisions and their ethical implications, and he gradually became aware of that course's overall significance for the Air Force Academy. He came to define that significance as the development of a new type of public servant in uniform who must serve the security interests of the country while grappling with issues of legal and ethical responsibility for his or her decisions. It is an extremely demanding role—perhaps the most demanding of all in this new era, when military officers must deal with advanced technology and face daily decisions of increasing complexity.

The responsibility of educating military officers in this context is enormous. It requires sensitivity to the ambiguities and complexities of situations that they will be encountering. It is therefore essential that both the cadets, who are studying to become military officers and leaders, and their senior military officers, who are presenting them with the issues they will be facing, develop the capacity for critical thinking and serious reflection required when these complex decisions must be made. Taking on this educational task was the challenge that faced those who were preparing a Holocaust course in each of the three military academies.

Zev began his outreach to the military academies less than three years after he had helped Hayes to launch the first Holocaust course offered at a university with the support of the Holocaust Educational Foundation. The process varied in each of these academies according to their academic structure, but from the beginning Zev discovered a willingness to explore the possibility of introducing Holocaust studies in their curriculum. Although members of the Board of Directors were getting accustomed to Zev's surprising moves, this one had them completely enthralled. They immediately understood that this was an opportunity to present a powerful historical reality to future military commanders who might well have to face situations with similar ethical implications. There was no hesitation on their part in giving Zev full support.

The United States Air Force Academy

From the perspective of the military academy faculty members interviewed who had been contacted by Zev, perhaps the most hesitant at first was Brigadier General Carl Reddel, chairman of the history department at the Air Force Academy in Colorado. Through years of experience, Reddel had become wary of individuals who attempted to reach the military academies with their personal, political, or religious agendas in order to influence the country's future leaders. When Zev called him to make an appointment, he crisply requested that Zev meet him at the officer's club at six o'clock in the morning. Zev flew to Colorado Springs and arrived at the meeting on time. From this first contact, Reddel could immediately see that he was dealing with a man whose only agenda was "largely, transcendentally, impressively humanitarian." He found Zev to be self-effacing, modest, genuine, and transparent in the best sense of the word. "If he had not been those things, if I had sensed that he had a self-serving agenda—personally or politically—I would have backed off." In Zev's words, "I got there on time and we hit it off."

A complicated and arduous procedure was required for the Air Force Academy to consider the introduction of a Holocaust course. Reddel, aware of what lay ahead, suggested that Zev call him back in a year and he would have an answer. Although Zev had already gotten used to a more speedy procedure, he accepted the offer and waited a year before he called back. When they met a year later, Reddel was ready to move. During that year, he had consulted with Professor Gerhard Weinberg, who was a visiting professor at the academy, about how to prepare for such a course. They decided to send Edward Westermann, an Air Force officer who had been recruited to the faculty of the Air Force Academy as a European studies specialist, to study at the University of Nebraska with Professor Alan Steinweis, a former student of Weinberg's. As a highly respected commissioned officer, Westermann was chosen by Reddel because he was determined that the course, with its emotionally charged material, be taught well and professionally.

According to Reddel, another important factor in the course development was the presence in Colorado Springs of Professor Dennis Showalter, an excellent military historian and a specialist on Germany teaching at Colorado College. Showalter agreed to serve as senior scholar and advisor for the course while Westermann was developing his specialized academic credentials. Once the appropriate faculty had been recruited, the course had to be prepared for curricular review, first within the history department and then by the professors and faculty of the Air Force Council. In the meantime, Reddel attended the second Lessons and Legacies Conference, which was held at Northwestern University in the fall of 1992. He came to the conference with unresolved concerns about the possible multiple agendas that could be brought to such a course with regard to contemporary issues. The temptations to rewrite history or to establish a political agenda were clearly potential hazards with such an emotional subject. However, when he saw the level of scholarship and the commitment to professionalism on the part of the academics at the conference, he came away assured that the Academy would ultimately benefit from this project.

One of the results of his experience at the Lessons and Legacies Conference, where he also met representatives from the other military academies, was a decision to create a course that would be as interdisciplinary as possible. During its first year the course would be offered on an experimental basis within the history department, and faculty from the literature, philosophy, ethics, and international law departments would be asked to participate. If the course succeeded, the following year Reddel would move the course to the humanities division, where it would assume a broader base in the institution. By moving it to the humanities division, Reddel then made it more readily available to cadets from many different majors, although the history department continued to play a dominant role and provided the course chairmanship. This procedure ultimately required a broader academic review, but the course proved successful, and the review ultimately took place. The course appeared in the catalog as part of the general humanities division, and over the years it has been taught by a number of graduate student recruits under the ongoing supervision of Showalter. These graduate students have each been handpicked to develop a long-term expertise on Holocaust studies and have pursued their doctoral degrees in that field.

The first year was a successful one, and by the second year, there were fifty-three cadets enrolled in a course that was capped at fifty. This was an exceptionally large enrollment for an upper-division elective course, since cadets have an extremely heavy schedule that includes far more math, physics, chemistry, biology, and electrical and civil engineering than students experience from the humanities departments at other universities. The course was split into four divisions: a historical background to anti-Semitism and the pre-Nazi regime era; the coming to power of the Nazi regime; the Holocaust itself; and then the post-Holocaust era with its displaced persons, the establishment of Israel, the war crimes trials, and current issues of genocide. The team of interdisciplinary instructors included faculty from philosophy, law, literature, art, and music, and the course covered forty lessons. This team teaching heightened the awareness of students and faculty alike to issues involved in the Holocaust.

Showalter continued to play a crucial role in conceptualizing the course and in helping with the teaching. The bibliography, which was chosen with great care, included Leni Yahil's *Holocaust: The Fate of European Jewry, 1932–1945,* which focuses on the perspectives, beliefs, and efforts of the various European Jewish communities; Donald Niewyk's *Holocaust,* which provides an anthology of the current Holocaust debates; and Christopher Browning's *Ordinary Men: Reserve Police Battalion 101 and the Final Solution in Poland,* which is particularly relevant for cadets who operate in a hierarchical context of authority and obedience.

The course format encouraged role playing and an open exchange of ideas, and there were four written assignments in which the dilemmas faced by both victims and perpetrators were addressed. The cadets were asked to write these assignments from the perspectives of a German Jew in 1938, an Orthodox Polish Jew in 1940, a Wehrmacht officer attached to the reserve police battalion in 1942, and a midlevel U.S. State Department official in late 1942. Through these assignments, the students were able to understand the complexity of the situations in which these people found themselves, to empathize with those who were caught in situations of terror, and to understand the significance of taking personal responsibility for making moral decisions on the part of those who are under military discipline. Related to the readings and role playing, there were classroom debates on the intentionalist and functionalist positions (which will be discussed in a later chapter), discussions on the role of Jewish councils, on forms of Jewish resistance, and an extended discussion on the question of Allied rescue, which was particularly relevant for future Air Force pilots. During the second year, Zev came to speak to the class, and his presentation was a powerful culmination of the course for students and faculty alike.

According to Lieutenant Colonel Lorrie Fenner, who took over the course organization, the impact of the course on the cadets was profound. She then added, "I think for me specifically with this audience it was important that they understand the many facets of human behavior and history. Things were not just historical occurrences but are part of who we are."

Fenner was not aware of any opposition on the part of the faculty, who were almost all military officers, to questions raised regarding military obedience. "Most of the instructors that I am a colleague with agree with me that it's important to make [the cadets] question their certainties when they are students, rather than when they are faced with real situations. So, among the colleagues that I have, it was an understood thing that officers have to make those moral choices all the time, and that pretending that we don't is criminal if you're trying to train young people and teach young people. There are some people who will always be uncomfortable with, let's say, people being able to think for themselves, to question. None of them complained or argued with me. You know, part of our mission is to create thinking human beings, and we talk a lot about critical thinking. So if anybody was opposed, for them to make any overt opposition apparent, they would have had to argue against our mission of teaching critical thinking and trying to help students develop character. So if anybody did have hard feelings, I don't think that it would have become public."

Captain Rondall Rice was the third officer to take over the Holocaust course after the two previous instructors, Westermann and Fenner, had left to continue their graduate studies. He had been stationed in Germany for a number of years and was interested primarily in studying military history when he applied to Reddel for a position in the history department at the Air Force Academy. Reddel knew that he would need someone for the Holocaust course and requested that Rice's master's thesis, which he was planning with Steinweis at the University of Nebraska, be on something related to the Holocaust. As an Air Force officer, he chose to work on the Auschwitz bombing controversy, and his interest in Holocaust related issues has continued.

Steinweis put Rice in contact with Zev and the Holocaust Educational Foundation, and Rice was invited to attend the first session of the Institute on Holocaust and Jewish Civilization, as well as the Lessons and Legacies Conferences that followed. The Air Force then sent Rice to the University of North Carolina at Chapel Hill for his doctoral studies, with a commitment to return and teach at the Academy on completion of his dissertation. Rice's assumption is that with his background and experience in the course, he will continue to teach Holocaust studies at the Academy when he returns. The course is thus assured continuity with a military professional who is well acquainted with its complexity, its multidisciplined approach, and its strong impact on all those involved.

The United States Military Academy at West Point

At West Point the tradition of dealing with the nature of higher orders and their morality has been incorporated into the curriculum for approximately two decades, and the Holocaust course was from the beginning viewed as an extension of that issue. There is also a carefully developed system of nine nonacademic goals for the entire process of educating future leaders in the military. Each activity is weighed in relation to these goals, and the Holocaust was found to be directly related to at least three of them: historical perspective, understanding human behavior, and cultural awareness. The ethical aspects of military command were incorporated into the outlook of the academy from its earliest years almost two centuries ago but were formalized during the Civil War in a code of honor and a program of ethical training. This program is now called the Value Education Training program. It includes compulsory weekly sessions in which small groups of cadets, led by fellow cadets, discuss ethical issues related to honor, consideration for others, and mutual respect. General Douglas MacArthur, a West Point graduate, is generally regarded as the embodiment of this code of honor.

As with the Air Force Academy, Zev first communicated in 1991 with the head of the West Point history department, Professor Robert Doughty. He in turn called in Professor Dewey Browder, acting head of the European division of the history department. Browder, a historian specializing in post–World War II Germany, already had a full load of courses and was also concerned that he did not know enough about the topic to teach it well. Zev offered to provide him with assistance in the acquisition of books for the library and with help that enabled Browder to make the necessary preparations. First Zev obtained the assistance of Hayes, who at that time was working in New York City at the Leo Baeck Institute. Hayes was willing to go to West Point for a day to offer suggestions about teaching approaches, a bibliography, and the development of a course syllabus. Second, Zev secured the support of a coinstructor who helped develop and teach the course. Professor Jack Wertheimer, from the Jewish Theological Seminary in New York City, began to make weekly trips to West Point—visits that continued through the years.

The first Holocaust course taught at that point was a small one, with five advanced-level students. This provided a framework for considerable student-faculty interaction, and the course was evaluated highly by the students. In the spring of 1993 the Foundation provided funding for the students to travel to Europe and visit Holocaust sites—a trip that added new dimensions to their experience. According to Browder, the course had particular relevance to these future officers who were "going to be in situations where they will be giving orders, and they are likely to be in situations where they'll be following orders. I think there's a cognizance that is cultivated by the fact that there can be illegal and immoral orders given. So I think they are better prepared after having that course . . . to deal with the vagaries of what goes on in a combat environment or in a war environment. We usually wind up with a discussion dealing with the nature of orders, and higher orders. If they are immoral and they are wrong, you don't follow them."

Browder has since moved to Tennessee, where he teaches at Austin Peay University. He has students in his classes who are in the Reserve Officers' Training Corps (ROTC) and will become military officers on completion of their degrees. Browder, who has continued to teach a course on the Holocaust, remains conscious of the value issues that are raised in the course and of their importance for these future officers. He is convinced that in the military, "They do everything they can at West Point, or wherever they're teaching the officers, to inculcate the importance of the value system, of humanity."

When Browder left West Point, Professor Lee Wyatt took over the teaching of the course, with the ongoing help of Wertheimer. Wyatt had become interested in Holocaust-related issues from previous contacts with Lorraine Beitner, a local historian. She had helped to set up an endowment for an annual spring bus trip for cadets to the United States Holocaust Memorial Museum in Washington, D.C., as well as a yearly Holocaust memorial service at West Point. Prior to teaching the course, Wyatt joined the Foundation's second Eastern European Study Seminar in 1997 and also attended the Institute on

Holocaust and Jewish Civilization during its two-week summer course. He has also attended two of the Lessons and Legacies Conferences and is convinced that because American soldiers are facing difficult problems in the Balkans, Africa, and elsewhere, it is particularly important for future officers to learn about the Holocaust.

The senior-level course, which he has developed over the years, includes the writing of a senior thesis on some aspect of the Holocaust. At one of the Holocaust memorial ceremonies, a cadet who had been chosen to make a presentation spoke of how her study of the Holocaust and her visit to the Holocaust Memorial Museum had been the most memorable experiences she had during her four years as a cadet. In 1999 one of the cadets won a national history honors award for the senior thesis he wrote on the Holocaust. Wyatt is convinced that the cadets' study of the Holocaust, an event that occurred "in the supposedly civilized twentieth century, heightens their awareness of how significant their role is when they go out and deal with people that have different backgrounds, different cultures, religions, different perspectives, and that sort of thing." Wyatt believes that as agents of the federal government and as military officers, they are called to higher standards. This call is reinforced by sending these young men and women to "represent the ideals that we're talking about" in current situations where genocide and cultural differences have become paramount issues.

Wyatt continues, "I think if you look at the role of the Academies, our mission is to educate and inspire [the cadets] for a lifetime of service to the nation whether that is as a military officer or when they get out and work in some other aspect. They have been given a special charge to give back to the nation, and for them to understand all these various issues is very important. They are going to be responsible for young men and women that are under their charge. They have to be able to understand all of the environment that they are in, in order to train, educate, and inspire those young men and women that are going to work for them as privates, specialists, and sergeants. They are going to be thrown into different environments."

The United States Naval Academy at Annapolis

Unlike at the other two military academies, the Holocaust course at Annapolis has been taught by the same professor, Larry Thompson, since its inception in 1992. As a higher-level elective taught in conjunction with Thompson's course on Germany and the Nazi experience, it has attracted over seventy midshipmen each year, an exceptionally large number for an elective course. Thompson has participated in all the Lessons and Legacies Conferences since 1992, joined the first East European Study Seminar, and attended the summer Institute on Holocaust and Jewish Civilization. He is acutely aware of the significance of his course in the Annapolis curriculum. Since the Academy is "an institution both educating and training individuals to become officers in the Navy and in the Marine Corps," Thompson believes that the course has much to teach about the necessity for public servants to take responsibility for their decisions.

In his course Thompson stresses the fact that all those who planned and executed the atrocities that they are studying were public servants who claimed to be doing their jobs. When in the mid-1990s there were some highly publicized incidents related to sexual harassment and car theft at Annapolis, the Academy's interest in the inculcation of ethical standards was heightened. There was an awareness that "a course such as the Holocaust is tailor made, in terms of the ethical consequences and implications derived from it." According to Thompson, "What has happened, at least here in the Academy, is that we now have a department in what we call professional development area, which is labeled 'Leadership and Law.' They do a great deal. They want the students to be exposed to aspects of this, particularly the excuse of superior orders. We also have established an Ethics Institute here at the Academy, with a director and so forth, funded by private funds from alumni who are interested in the Holocaust from an ethical perspective."

This newly created program of the Ethics Institute, which is compulsory for all midshipmen, includes required readings that lead to discussions about the ethical ramifications involved in leadership decisions. Thompson is frequently used as a resource for this program, and he has recommended that excerpts from Christopher Browning's book *Ordinary Men* become part of these required readings. Thompson believes that the program of ethics has now become well integrated into the life of the academy: "In part it's been because of the impact of the Holocaust, and in part it's been by our behavior."

To summarize, it seems clear that Zev Weiss and the Holocaust Educational Foundation have had a significant impact on an important aspect of life at the three major military academies in the United States. As the Foundation's treasurer Howard Stone pointed out, a forum has been created in these academies in which the lessons of the Holocaust can be taught to the future military leadership of the country. "Who knows what impact that will have on people that are making command decisions during wartime? [It is an] impact not on Jews, but Bosnians, or Vietnamese. Genocide is genocide." Stone believes that these courses on the Holocaust are serving to "raise the level of humanity within individuals of the general population, and with people that find themselves in positions of command in the future. How can one measure the impact? The chief of staff, or a field commander, a guy in the field, making a decision, will be impacted by the lessons that were learned during the Holocaust studies course when he or she was twenty-one years old."

Finally, there have been some unexpected ramifications for military institutions that go beyond the three military academies. Throughout the country many ROTC members on college campuses have participated in general Holocaust courses encouraged by the Foundation. More specifically, Fenner, who taught for one year at the Air Force Academy and is continuing to pursue her degree in a Holocaust-related field, is preparing a syllabus for a Holocaust course to be given at the National War College. This is a graduate institution for senior military officers, as well as State Department and other government officials. It is the program that is recommended for those who are slated to become generals, admirals, or ambassadors. When delivering a lecture there, Fenner found considerable interest in this subject, and she hopes that she will be asked to teach the course she is preparing. Zev Weiss and the Foundation have been instrumental in helping to expose the military leaders of the United States to the Holocaust and the ethical lessons to be learned from it.

The Developing Field of Holocaust Studies

ONLY AFTER A SLOW HISTORICAL EVOLUTION WAS THE HOLOCAUST—
the destruction of one-third of the world's Jewry—recognized as one
of the major events of the twentieth century. The process of how that
recognition evolved has now become a specialized field in Holocaust
studies. Raul Hilberg was the first historian in the Western world to
produce a comprehensive study of how the Nazi regime carried out
the systematic murder of so many millions of human beings. In his
opening address at the Foundation's first Lessons and Legacies Conference in 1989, which was published together with the papers given
at that conference by Northwestern University Press, Hilberg described the process of how the Holocaust was "discovered" by the
world. These remarks were then expanded into an autobiographical
book whose title (*The Politics of Memory: The Journey of a Holocaust
Historian*) suggests some of the influences on that process of discovery and recognition. It is a process that has been reflected in the life
story of Zev Weiss, who in turn has had a profound influence on that
process through the activities of the Foundation.

When Zev arrived in Canada as a teenager, no one was interested
in hearing what had happened to him and his family during the war
years. Hilberg had great difficulty finding a university willing to em-
ploy a Jewish historian who had become the world expert on the destruction of European Jewry. It took many years to find a publisher
for his book, which finally was printed in a limited edition, but its
main flowcharts were distorted, and it went largely unreviewed and
unnoticed by the wider public.

Some historians attribute the failure to acknowledge the Holocaust to the deliberate policies of Western governments, which were
far more interested in demonizing the Soviet Union at the start of

the Cold War. Others attributed it to the need of Jews in Israel and around the world for heroism and their horror at acknowledging the role of Jews as victims. Hilberg, however, emphasizes the almost universal need among human beings to disbelieve what is both traumatic and incomprehensible. This disbelief began with the victims themselves, who were already isolated in ghettos under conditions of severe deprivation, and who heard persistent rumors of the fate awaiting them. How can any human being raised within the context of a civilized society and taught to trust that despite life's real hardships, people do have some control over their fate, believe that they would be deliberately killed even though they had neither committed crimes nor been in direct conflict with some enemy? How could they grasp that the German government was determined to eliminate every man, woman, and child whom it defined as Jewish?

Decades passed before such deeply rooted disbelief was questioned and before the events surrounding the destruction of European Jewry became an acknowledged subject for historical scholarship and public interest. Even now there are deniers who maintain that the events that have been so carefully documented and chronicled did not occur. Until the Eichmann trial in 1961, most books and articles dealing with the events of the Second World War barely mentioned the destruction of European Jewry. Most historians, however, credit that trial in Israel for first breaking the public silence. The intricate process of how that breakthrough was then used for one political agenda or another is still being studied, as are many aspects of the Holocaust itself. With such a major subject involving all of Europe, most of the countries in the Western world, and many others around the globe that either granted or denied entry to the fleeing refugees, there are still many important Holocaust-related subjects that remain unexplored.

The subject of the perpetrators was the first to interest both scholars and the general public. How could one group of human beings do this to another group? How could this take place in the civilized world when those who were targeted for the Final Solution were men, women, and children who were unarmed, who were living their lives within communities scattered throughout Europe, and who were not politically or militarily involved in opposition to those who decided to murder them systematically? Generally, the finger of blame would be pointed to Adolf Hitler himself as the source and epitome of evil. This answer, however, turned out to be too facile, and, as will be seen, teachers of Holocaust courses on university campuses find that seeking easy answers is one of the major obstacles they face with their students. It has taken a generation for German and other historians painstakingly to collect evidence demonstrating that the story of the perpetrators is far more complex. It is a story that most of these scholars believe to have great relevance for students in today's bureaucratic and corporate world.

Subsequently, the victims and bystanders began to draw attention and scholarship. How did they resist their fate? How do human beings live under conditions of such extreme deprivation? What was the nature of the richly traditional East European Jewish civilization that had been destroyed? And what happened both to the scattered remnants of European Jewry that survived and to world Jewry as a result of this tragedy? Bystanders were neither perpetrators nor victims but those who knew about the fate of the Jews and mainly did nothing. A growing body of scholars began to document the lack of response of individuals, organizations, and even countries to the Holocaust, as well as the instances of heroic rescue.

Hilberg, Marrus, and other scholars point to the second half of the 1970s as a turning point in terms of general public interest and awareness of the Holocaust in North America. The term *Holocaust* itself was becoming widely used to describe what had happened. According to David Hackett, professor of German history at the University of Texas in El Paso, "In order for an event to be a historical event, it has to have a name. And we didn't have a name for it. Until then, without such an accepted term, it could not be placed in the chronology of history." In addition, many millions had seen a number of media events, including a television series on a German Jewish family during the early years of persecution. There was a growing awareness that those who had survived the Holocaust were getting older, and that eyewitness testimonies would soon be scarce. Individuals like Zev Weiss found that the stories that no one had formerly wanted to hear were now being eagerly sought out. Around the world there were other organizations, like the Holocaust Educational Foundation, as yet generally unaware of one another but beginning to gather information from survivors on audiocassettes and videocassettes. In North America Yale's Fortunoff Video Archive for Holocaust Testimonies was instrumental in raising the consciousness of many communities about the importance of preserving these testimonials for posterity.

A few academics began to highlight Holocaust-related events in their university courses during the 1970s, and there were even a few who had begun to offer a full course on the Holocaust as part of their teaching load. It was still not known how the academic world would receive such courses and whether they would be approved as part of the ongoing departmental curriculum. Graduate students who were interested in researching some part of this subject were warned by their advisors that there was no guarantee that they would find a job in the academic world when their dissertations were completed. However, recognition moved steadily ahead during the 1980s, and with the wide success of Steven Spielberg's film *Schindler's List* in the early 1990s, Holocaust studies had become a recognized field of study. There are many theories of how such widespread recognition came about in America, including Novick's controversial accusations of media manipulation by Jewish interest groups.

By the time that Zev and the Holocaust Educational Foundation began their outreach to academics around the country, universities were generally prepared to approve such a course in their departmental offerings if a member of the faculty wanted to teach it. In a sense, the academic field was ready for such an outreach. It was a moment when Zev's long-deferred vision and the educational arena in which he had dreamed of implementing that vision could come together in a project that would succeed in enriching the lives of hundreds of academicians and many thousands of university students.

A reflection of the change in public interest was the fact that none of the academics interviewed who were spurred to offer a course on the Holocaust through Zev's outreach found procedural obstacles specifically related to the course contents that needed to be overcome in their universities. Virtually all those interviewed who introduced Holocaust courses after contact with Zev and with the Foundation claimed that there had been no serious resistance to the introduction of the course at their universities. In fact, by the time Professor Johnpeter Horst Grill introduced his course at Mississippi State University in 1996, it was almost taken for granted that no opposition would be forthcoming. Surprised, and perhaps somewhat offended at the question of opposition to the course or obstacles encountered,

Grill replied, "Absolutely not. Nothing but support from administration, department head. I can't imagine where you would find that unless you go into the sticks somewhere. You know the South is not *Mississippi Burning* anymore." There were even two professors—Donald McKale at Clemson University in South Carolina and Doris Bergen, currently at Notre Dame but originally at the University of Vermont—who both felt that their ability to teach about the Holocaust was an important factor in their being hired by the university. Apparently, the seemingly insurmountable obstacles that Zev had encountered during the mid-1980s when he first began approaching universities about introducing the course no longer existed.

In the last years of the century another important development occurred. Except for Saul Friedlander's Chair in Holocaust Studies at the University of California–Los Angeles, the subject had not yet made the jump from undergraduate studies to major research universities and the training of the next generation of doctoral candidates. By the end of the century, however, Clark University had a doctoral program in Holocaust studies; Northwestern University had the Theodore Zev Weiss Holocaust Educational Foundation Chair in Holocaust Studies where Hayes was teaching; and there were several major research universities where Holocaust studies had gained standing. Omer Bartov at Brown University and Christopher Browning at the University of North Carolina at Chapel Hill had both joined graduate research faculties where Holocaust specialization was considered an advantage, rather than the liability it had been for many years.

There were, however, some more subtle manifestations of resistance that were neither official nor bureaucratic. According to Peter Hayes, "In academia of the 1980s in certain leftish quarters, it was fashionable to identify with Palestinian nationhood and, therefore, to be mistrustful of the subject of the Holocaust as a way of making people feel guilty about the past, and exonerating Israel in the present. I knew it was there. I heard snippets of it. I got a sense of its existence. But it never came up in the form of something that I had to fight." In addition, there were those who asked, "Why talk about that atrocity in the twentieth century? Why not talk about some other atrocity?" Hayes was aware of some people who "muttered in the background, 'Why are we not looking at American imperialism and the Khmer Rouge?' However, I never encountered any problems at Northwestern. I won't say that there were not mistrustful people around. There were."

Other versions of this problem were also described. Professor Arnold Kramer at Texas A&M heard a rumor that questioned why the course he was proposing highlighted the Jews when other people had also been killed. There were those who wanted to know why his course did not relate to a "Holocaust of people, not just Jews." In this same vein, David Murphy, a professor of history at Anderson University in Indiana, had some difficulty with the name of his proposed course. The curriculum committee requested that he change "The Holocaust 1933–1945" to "The Jewish Holocaust." The name that was finally agreed upon, which was not of Murphy's choosing, was "Jewish Holocaust in Its Historical Context." Professor Marvin Swartz was also asked to change the name of his course: "I had colleagues who insisted that there were other holocausts—dropping the atomic bomb on the Japanese, or other massacres of people elsewhere—and they were doubtful whether I should call it a history of the holocaust. But I got my way. I told them that anti-Semites might not like it, and they got the point."

The only serious issue raised in one place was not from either the university administration or the faculty department, but rather from parts of the wider public. When the University of North Dakota announced that David Meier, professor of German history, had received a fellowship to take part in a study tour in order to prepare for a new course to be offered on the Holocaust, the Meier family began to receive obscene phone calls each evening. They had to change their phone number and remove it from the directory. Meier also received in the mail a lengthy venomous letter about his contribution to Jewish conspiracies. This, however, was the only known occurrence of such a hate campaign.

The courses were generally welcomed wherever they were offered. Strangely enough, it was the very success and popularity of the Holocaust courses that became something of an obstacle. Professor Kees Gispen at the University of Mississippi began to hear some murmurings against the course from colleagues in the history department because it was regularly attracting students away from other course offerings, particularly those related to German history. Although the administration was pleased with the large enrollment, those German historians who were left behind began to grumble about the relevance of the course. German history, they asserted, was becoming associated with the Nazi era and the Holocaust, and many German historians were not happy about this development. There were rumblings about the purposeful manipulation of history by Jewish interests, and these rumblings were certainly reinforced in 1999 with the publication of Novick's strident, controversial book *The Holocaust in American Life*. Novick claims that an awareness of the Holocaust was artificially grafted onto the consciousness of Americans by Jewish organizations with a political agenda.

Compared to other books that appeared in the 1990s and attempted to analyze the fascination with the Holocaust in American culture, Novick's stance was particularly negativistic. Michael Marrus, professor of history at the University of Toronto, indicates the dangers of the Holocaust's entry into "the bloodstream of American popular culture" through the mass media in his article titled "The Use and Misuse of the Holocaust." These dangers include the oversimplification, inaccuracy, misrepresentation, and trivialization of the growing body of Holocaust research in the service of media fads and the manipulation of political and commercial interests. There are many examples to prove that these dangers have materialized, and they have led some scholars to express concern over the spread of Holocaust courses on campuses throughout the country. It is an issue that had been given considerable thought by most of the academics interviewed.

Although the dangers are clearly recognized, most of those teaching Holocaust courses believe that it is a subject that must continue to be studied. Professors Christopher Browning (University of North Carolina), Donald Schilling (Dennison University), Roger Brooks (Connecticut College), Steven Katz (Boston University), Karl Schleunes (University of North Carolina), Rebecca Boehling (University of Maryland), Geoffrey Giles (University of Florida), Steven Hochstadt (Bates College), Doris Bergen (Notre Dame), and many others agree that, for Americans, the Holocaust has become recognized as a central event in modern historical experience and a key to understanding much of what happened in the twentieth century. At this point, it would be unthinkable to turn back the clock and once again marginalize its significance in history. In addition, the course material dramatizes ideological issues that have immediate relevance for students in their various life contexts. As Hayes pointed out, the events took place in a Western, Christian, literate, and industrialized country that had previously had a parliamentary democracy, if only for a short period. It is easier for Americans to identify with events that took place in such a context than, for instance, with Stalin's massacres, which occurred in a place seen as backward and totalitarian, or with the Armenians who were slaughtered by the Ottoman Empire, which had an Islamic culture.

In his thoughtful article published in Helene Flanzbaum's *Americanization of the Holocaust,* Alan Steinweis, professor of history at the University of Nebraska, describes how Holocaust awareness developed in Nebraska, a Midwestern state with relatively few Jews and a large population descended from German immigrants. He attributes the widespread interest in the Holocaust to its general acceptance as a paradigm of human evil in the twentieth century. Since this evil, which was perpetrated across the ocean, was one that the United States helped to destroy, Americans have a sense of righteousness toward it. In addition, Steinweis feels that particularly in an area with Germanic roots, there is a good deal of guilt associated with the role of both Germany and of the Christian church. By studying the Holocaust, some students are attempting to "cleanse their Christian faith."

This theme of concern for the role of the Christian church was often raised by those interviewed as a partial explanation for the widespread interest in Holocaust studies on college campuses. In particular, those who were teaching at Church-sponsored universities like Whitworth College and Pacific Lutheran University in Washington or Notre Dame and Anderson University in Indiana stressed the deep concern expressed by students on this issue. This concern, however, was only one aspect of the broader moral issues that find expression in the context of a Holocaust course. Although there is a universal, sometimes prurient fascination with evil in all its manifestations, students often show a real desire to wrestle with the issues related to man's capacity for cruelty and for inflicting unspeakable harm on other human beings.

This need to find answers to the key moral and ethical questions of the twentieth and twenty-first centuries is perhaps most often cited as the reason for the consistent popularity of Holocaust courses. The main existential questions concerning how life is lived and how choices are made by each human being during his or her lifetime are legitimately raised by students when the events of the Holocaust are presented. And these are indeed the questions that are consistently raised on every campus where these courses are taught. Whether these questions are reserved for an end-of-semester summation or are discussed throughout the course, they are part of every Holocaust course. Since there is a limited number of courses offered at any university that afford an opportunity for such discussion, and since the quest for answers to moral concerns is virtually universal, it is not difficult to see why Holocaust courses have such widespread appeal. Many young people search for intellectual challenges and for answers to their questions about moral choices. Both of these needs are generally met in the context of university Holocaust courses, so it is no wonder that the interest in these courses has been sustained.

Although there are still those who question the relevance of Holocaust studies on college campuses in America, it appears to be a process that is not likely to be reversed. Despite the many vulgarizations and distortions inherent in the "Americanization of the Holocaust," years of careful scholarship are continuing to make what happened available to serious scholars around the world, and it seems likely that the Holocaust will remain what it has now become: something that happened to Jews but is relevant to nearly everyone.

At the hundreds of universities where Holocaust courses are now offered, not all those teaching these courses are doing so because of Zev and the Holocaust Educational Foundation. A few individuals had begun to teach before Zev's outreach, and others have since come into the field without direct contact with the Foundation. But there is no doubt that Zev Weiss and his Foundation have had a major impact on both the quantity and the quality of Holocaust studies in colleges and universities throughout the country.

The Academic Courses on the Holocaust: Content and Emphasis

DESPITE THE EVER-GROWING INTEREST IN HOLOCAUST STUDIES AT IN-
stitutions of higher education, there are, as mentioned, still some critics who oppose the spread of Holocaust studies in colleges and universities. According to Novick, there is little for Americans to learn
from the Holocaust since they are bombarded daily with media im-
ages of murder, bombings, and atrocities and do not need to be re-
minded that there is evil in the world. He argues that the term *Holocaust* itself has been adopted by every organization that feels itself
aggrieved, including antiabortionists and animal rights groups, so
whatever lessons there are to be learned from the Holocaust are by
now either politicized, sentimentalized, or useless.

The many scholars and academics teaching Holocaust studies on
college campuses clearly disagree with this critique that has been
hurled in their direction. Among these scholars are historians, phil-
osophers, sociologists, theologists, psychologists, and political scientists, as well as professors of literature and Judaic studies. As will
be seen, their perspectives vary, but many themes are common to all
these disciplines because Holocaust studies is an interdisciplinary
field. Although the history of the Third Reich and of the Second
World War form the foundation on which most Holocaust courses
are built, even historians of modern Germany agree that they must
refer to many other disciplines, including literature, psychology, Judaic studies, and political science in order to convey a more complete
picture of what occurred. The subject of the Holocaust is vast. Every area of life was affected for the tens of millions of individuals throughout the European continent and beyond who were connected directly and indirectly with the events as they unfolded.

Scholars are uncovering new information and gaining new insights that add new dimensions to all that is already known.

One of the more salient challenges facing academics teaching Holocaust courses is dealing judiciously with representations and misrepresentations from the mass media that students bring with them and the general tendency in the American culture to seek quick and easy answers to complex issues. Most students come into class assuming that they already know what will be taught. This dilemma is presented by Marjorie Lamberti, a professor of German history at Middlebury College in Vermont, who had been teaching Holocaust courses before she became involved with the Foundation's various projects. She found that dealing with these issue became increasingly more challenging over the years: "So what I had to do in my class is, one might say, not discredit the misrepresentations of the Holocaust in the media, but to bring my students up to a higher level of understanding. And that is a big challenge. You really have to work often against the knowledge that they've acquired in the media about the Holocaust. Some of it is so oversimplified."

Professor Lamberti's solution is to maintain a sense of respect for this popular knowledge despite its superficiality: "I think it's important that scholars not debunk popular culture. It's a reality. But I think that what we have to do is to show our students that there's something more complex, something deeper. And there are many rewards in historical understanding. The very fact that books and films draw such a wide public indicates that for many people the Holocaust has become the benchmark of human evil at its extremity of cruelty and sadism. And I think there is that curiosity, that quest for some kind of tidy, packaged information that is going to continue. But I think that we historians . . . should take on the challenge and find pedagogical strategies to give our students. To bring our students to another level of historical understanding." Understandably, there is initial resistance to this solution. However, most students eventually respond well to the fact that they are being asked to stretch their intellects and overthrow artificial props that have restrained them from deeper analysis of important issues that are relevant to their lives.

Professor Donald Schilling from Dennison University in Ohio illustrates how this challenge can be faced: "The students come into class at different levels of background in knowledge, and definitely one of my goals is to help them understand the more complicated issues of historical background, of the nature of the state and how that functioned, the range of victim experience, the range of responses to the different situations, the bystanders' behavior, the issues of historical legacy, the consequences of the Holocaust in our contemporary world. I want to expand their understanding of what the Holocaust is in a significant way. So there is that fundamental goal of opening up horizons of knowledge. A second goal is to help students understand that there is not a single narrative to the Holocaust. There are multiple narratives. These narratives are a product not only of different types of experience, but also of different interpretations, different understanding of different acts. In the Holocaust there are areas where there is a historical debate about interpretation. And that is deepening their understanding of history—that history is not just a single narrative, that the facts don't just speak for themselves. This is true for other scholarly disciplines. There are certain answers that will come out of a discipline given the methodology that is used. Given the perspective of the scholar, etc. So they should be aware of the factors shaping the narratives. To be better able to understand what helped shape them."

This search for deeper historical understanding was widely echoed by those interviewed. In order to illustrate how this can be achieved, Professor Dagmar Herzog from Michigan State University described a process of "layering" that took place during the semester. She offered a description of how she teaches her course to provide some insight into the process of gradually deepening understanding: "I teach twice a week. I give a lecture on some issue, like different theories on perpetrator motivation, or how those theories evolved over time. And then they'll have a discussion where they'll read different historians about perpetrators and some primary documents. Then I'll have them break into small groups and they write group reports on what they thought, so they are really having to struggle over the issues interpretively. I teach very high level intellectual scholarly readings, and sometimes the students are just overwhelmed by that. They want to just have the 'Nazis bad, Jews victims, end of story.' But then they have to come to terms with becoming intellectuals. Suddenly that's the drama for them, and it isn't even the Holocaust per se."

Herzog continues with the description of her course: "I start with anti-Semitism before the enlightenment . . . because that was my field. Just so they have some context. [The Holocaust] didn't come out of nowhere. Then Weimar Germany and the rise of Nazis and the context of German political history. And then I go through the Holocaust itself. . . . Nazi policies towards Jews and other 'undesirables.' And then warfare and the enormous part of the Holocaust that was shooting as opposed to the gas chambers. Then I do the concentration, labor, and extermination camps. So I suddenly have gotten through all the factual information really fast. . . . Then what happens is I end up getting to the interpretive issues. We do perpetrators, a lecture and a discussion; victims, a lecture and a discussion; bystanders, a lecture and a discussion. They then have to deal with all these primary sources. And then the history of memory in Germany. The extent to which Germans have come to terms with the Holocaust or not. So we are actually repeating the themes that we have been doing. We keep layering it. Then we do a theological perspective. It's quite a course. I feel like a dishrag at the end."

Conveying the complexity of historical data was also the main goal of Doris Bergen, professor of history at Notre Dame. It is important to her to convey to students that the Holocaust was an event that occurred within the chronology of twentieth-century history: "That may seem obvious, but I'm a historian. I taught my course as a history course, in the history department, and I think that a lot of times people know something vague about the Holocaust. They've heard about it; they know it's something they should feel bad about; but they don't understand how it fit into the history of Europe in the twentieth century. And I wanted the students to see that. This didn't happen on another planet. It wasn't carried out by some kind of brainwashed automatons or creatures from Mars. This was an event in human history. It had causes, and motivations, and results, and connections to other events before and afterwards. . . . In more subtle ways I wanted the students to see how complicated the Holocaust is and how many angles it can be studied from and needs to be studied from. So I set up the course with a lot of different kinds of materials. I had a lot of different kinds of readings and events put into the class to help the students understand both the magnitude of this event and the complexity of it."

One of the factors contributing to this complexity was brought to the attention of the academic world by Gerhard Weinberg, the distinguished professor at the University of North Carolina who became the mentor for many of the newer academics entering the field. As a well-published historian of the Nazi era, Weinberg became aware that in most of the research and publications about that era, World War II and the Holocaust were rarely studied together. They were seen as two completely separate entities, and still today there are books about the Second World War that do not mention Jews or the Holocaust and books about the Holocaust that do not mention the war. According to Weinberg, 95 percent of the Jewish victims would not have come under German control if not for the war. Weinberg's need to unify these two subjects gave him the impetus to make contact with Zev and the Holocaust Educational Foundation and to prepare a course on the Holocaust. His approach has influenced many professors, such as Donald McKale from Clemson University, South Carolina, who said that he had previously taught about the Holocaust as though it took place in a vacuum. He is now better able to connect the Holocaust with what was going on in Germany and with the Second World War.

For many decades the Holocaust survivor, author, and Nobel peace prize winner Elie Wiesel, who was the first and best-known spokesman on Holocaust issues, maintained that the Holocaust could never be comprehended, not even by those who had endured its sufferings. He was shocked by the growing popularization of the term, with its accompanying attempts to apply the concept to other manifestations of human brutality, and insisted on the Holocaust's uniqueness in human history. Although by any standards the destruction of European Jewry was indeed unique, for years that very uniqueness contributed to researchers' hesitation to study its many aspects carefully. However, the era of hesitation has passed, and scholars from many disciplines are studying the events themselves in all their complexities. The results of these studies are being made available to those who are teaching, and they in turn are conveying what they learn to their students.

Most professors are convinced that students can be brought to an understanding of Holocaust events without forfeiting either the complexity or the uniqueness of these events. Steinweis of the University of Nebraska believes that it is essential to heighten the intellectual grasp of students by presenting them with the facts: "I believe that there is nothing about the Holocaust that cannot be understood, using the intellectual tools that are available to us as scholars. I don't think that it is an event that is beyond normal historical understanding. It has its unique characteristics; that's undeniable. But that does not necessarily mean that we are somehow less able to understand it than we are slavery, or the Civil War, or World War I, or the Crusades, or whatever. So the primary goal of my course on the Holocaust is to enable the students to intellectually grasp what happened. I try to convey the basic story of what happened, but also to understand why it is that these events came to pass."

Why such a vast range of tragic events came to pass is certainly part of the complexity, and even those who have a firm grasp on the chronology of the events do not claim that there is one all-encompassing answer. Although all scholars would agree that Hitler's extreme hatred of the Jews was absolute and uncompromising, the weight given to the history of anti-Semitism in Germany prior to the Nazi era and to its impact on the emergence of Hitler's Final Solution varies according to the perspective of the lecturer. Beginning in the early 1980s, a debate was raging in the field concerning this issue, which came to be labeled the *functionalist-intentionalist controversy.*

Two issues were debated in this controversy: First, did Hitler make the key decisions, or did the Final Solution emerge piecemeal from below? Second, if Hitler did play the key role in the decision-making process, did he do so according to a long-held intention or plan logically derived from his ideology, or did he respond to changing circumstances and situations in ways that were consistent with his ideology and obsessive anti-Semitism but not according to some long-held plan or blueprint merely awaiting the opportune moment for implementation?

Lucy Davidowicz has been the most extreme advocate of what could be called *ultraintentionalism,* that is, the claim that Hitler knew since 1919 that he would murder the Jews. Gerald Fleming has been another key protagonist of the intentionalist camp. He has argued for a direct line from Hitler's early expressions to the death camps. Other less extreme intentionalists (e.g., Helmut Krausnick, Andreas Hillgruber) emphasized the key role of Hitler and his ideology, but they have not insisted dogmatically on some early, clear formation of a plan. Most recently, Richard Breitman has argued along what many now call *moderate intentionalist* lines that Hitler decided on the mass murder of the Jews in early 1941 as part of the planning for Barbarossa.

On the other hand, Martin Broszat and Hans Mommsen, in what has been called the *ultrafunctionalist* camp, have argued that there was neither a plan nor even a Hitler decision or order. The Final Solution emerged piecemeal from below and did not take on the shape of a systematic program for the total mass murder of the Jews until mid-1942. Others, like Karl Schleunes and Christopher Browning, have argued for a "twisted road" to Auschwitz. These *moderate functionalists* say that Hitler did play a central role, but he did not operate according to some long-held plan. He intended to solve his self-imposed Jewish question "one way or another" but did not know beforehand where that would lead him. What emerged was an evolution of Nazi Jewish policy through the stages of emigration, expulsion, and finally mass murder, with Hitler playing a key role in the decision-making process.

The new generation of German scholars is leaning more toward the functionalist end of the spectrum, with special emphasis on the role of local initiative and autonomy of the German occupiers in Poland and the Soviet Union in instigating the mass murder. One among them, Christian Gerlach, nonetheless argues for a specific Hitler "basic decision" at the relatively late date of December 1941.

Another controversy, triggered by Daniel Goldhagen in 1996 with the publication of his book titled *Hitler's Willing Executioners, Ordinary Germans, and the Holocaust,* has been over the weight to be given to pre-Nazi German anti-Semitism in the development of the Holocaust. Goldhagen's embrace of a strong intentionalist position came at a point when the research findings of the last two decades had led Holocaust scholars to modify their views. At this point, scholars embrace some form of synthesis and reject what is now called a false dichotomy.

The intensity of the intentionalist-functionalist controversy began to abate a decade after it began, and many of the professors interviewed have found that these positions can be more readily synthesized than was previously thought. Neither side minimizes the extent of Hitler's virulent anti-Semitism or underestimates its impact on the progression of events. Professor Ronald Smelser, who has been teaching Holocaust courses at the University of Utah since 1983, claims that his position from the beginning has been to attempt a synthesis between the functionalists and the intentionalists, who he feels are not unresolved opposites. And David Murphy at Anderson University believes that the dichotomy is a false one since there were clearly some individuals who intended for all the Jews to be killed from the beginning, while others were drawn into the destruction without original intent. Although some scholars still find themselves at one extreme or the other, most of those interviewed define themselves as either modified functionalists or modified intentionalists, with a range of variations in between.

Whether the Final Solution was predetermined or not, Professor Karl Schleunes at the University of North Carolina believes that a thorough exposure to the history of anti-Semitism in Germany is an essential feature of a Holocaust course. "I teach down in North Carolina, in what is called the Christian Bible Belt, and I think it's very important to introduce the students to the underside, or the dark side of Christianity, and its role in the development of anti-Jewish sentiment. So I spend about a half a semester tracing the history of anti-Semitism. This is all a background, which in a sense expands the Holocaust beyond an artifact, a horrible artifact of Germany. I think it's very important to take the consciousness of students and expand it beyond that. The first half of the semester deals with the long history of anti-Semitism and the coming to power of the Nazis, and then the second half of the semester deals with the horror of the Holocaust itself. And here again, I'm interested in expanding beyond the notion that this could only happen in Germany. I have the students read Christopher Browning's *Ordinary Men*. I try to get into the heads of the perpetrators and trace the development of the escalation and the destruction of the death camps."

Getting into the heads of those involved in the Holocaust events, whether perpetrators, victims, or bystanders, usually involves an interdisciplinary perspective when teaching a Holocaust course. However, one of the factors that influences the perspective from which a Holocaust course is taught is the academic context in which it is placed. Although it has been Zev's policy from the beginning to mainstream these courses within the general curriculum of the university through departments such as history or literature, there are a few universities that offer the course in their Judaic studies departments.

The advantage of such placement is that the course then generally offers a rich background of Judaism and how it was affected by the Holocaust, as well as a more comprehensive description of the culture of Eastern European Jewry that was destroyed. The disadvantage is that the course is often less likely to be chosen by the general student body. There are some universities that cross-list their

Holocaust course with various departments, often including Judaic studies. In the context of a department of religion or Judaic studies, Roger Brooks, professor of theology at Connecticut College, believes that a Holocaust course can offer a different perspective: "The first thing is, I do a lot of work with the students on religious implications of the Holocaust. So what does it mean to Christian theology if this happened in a Christian country? What does it mean to Jewish theology? What can we read out of simple things like the terms people use for the Holocaust? What kind of theological implications can we read out of that?"

Many of those interviewed were aware of the inadequacy in their scholastic background with regard to Jewish religion and Jewish civilization. As will be seen in a section devoted to this subject, the annual summer Institute on Holocaust and Jewish Civilization was established by the Holocaust Educational Foundation to address this problem. Those who attended the institute were then able to include information about European Jewry in their course. Steinweis (University of Nebraska), who was already knowledgeable on this subject, explained his position thus: "Because I teach the course at a university that has very, very few Jewish students, one goal that I set for myself was to use [the course] to convey some understanding of who Jews are and what Judaism is. A lot of students will take my course on the Holocaust who will not take any other course in Jewish studies here. I try to integrate some understanding of Jewish history and Judaism into it as well."

An understanding of Jewish history and of the theological implications of the Holocaust was one of the perspectives that varied in its saliency according to the academic discipline of the lecturer. The theoretical perspectives from which the issues were presented formed another. Since not all who teach Holocaust courses are historians, different perspectives are offered to students. Deborah Abowitz, professor of sociology at Bucknell University, is an ardent advocate for the introduction of sociological research into Holocaust studies. With an academic expertise in the study of social groupings, Abowitz, whose work is grounded in theories of collective behavior, poses questions about the processes in society that allow social movements to develop and to succeed. She questions what affects peoples' adherence to these movements, how it impacts their behavior, and whether that behavior becomes institutionalized. The questions she raises are both sociological and social psychological, and she is convinced that sociology, with its studies in group behavior and its subfield of disaster behavior, has a great deal to contribute to Holocaust studies. Although sociologists readily acknowledge their need for the work of historians, Abowitz believes that sociology has insights into patterns of group behavior with regard to perpetrators, bystanders, and victims that are rarely used or acknowledged by historians.

James Waller, a professor of psychology at Whitworth College in Spokane, Washington, brings the perspective of yet another discipline. He believes that there is much to learn about the psychology of the perpetrators, victims, and bystanders, although it is not a substitute for the insights of history, literature, philosophy, or theology. According to Waller, "What I want to do in the course is motivated by an understanding that a complete examination and understanding of the Holocaust and other cases of genocide are going to come from a lot of disciplinary perspectives." Waller, who teaches in an institution affiliated with the Presbyterian church, finds that many of his students are interested in the role of God and in why God did not intervene. To address these questions, he has introduced into his course a section on theodicy and the problem of evil. He then uses this section to focus the attention of the students on their own roles as bystanders. He poses various questions: "What are the ongoing cases of genocide or mass killing going on in the world today that we know about? What do we learn from the Holocaust in terms of bystander behavior that we could apply to our government today, to us, to our city, to our state, and so on? I think that leap is easier for them to make of recognizing their obligation as a citizen in a democracy to be heard about this issue whether it's here or anywhere around the world."

MORAL AND ETHICAL ISSUES IN COURSE CONTENT

Although almost all of those who were interviewed spoke either directly or indirectly about the moral lessons to be learned from a study of the Holocaust, using the Holocaust to learn about the obligations of citizenship is not without controversy. A university course is often expected to offer scientific objectivity. Is it also an appropriate forum to learn about ethics and morality? Can one rely on the facts that are presented to speak for themselves? Most of the members of the Board of Directors assume that the project they are supporting does address this issue either directly or indirectly. Jon Mills, an active board member, believes that a Holocaust course should be taught on every college campus: "I think it's pertinent to everybody on the face of the earth. You know, without getting religious. . . . I don't go to synagogue, so I'm not into that stuff, but certainly, we are each other's brothers. I'd like [students] to have an understanding of what can happen when society or humanity gets out of control. I don't know what the class says, but I would hope that one of the ending classes says that we do have a responsibility to prevent these situations in the future. I don't know if they say that. They probably don't. But maybe the kids are bright enough to deduce that themselves. You know, in this kind of class, your hope would be that it would influence, in a positive way, better behavior for the world of the future."

Most professors seem to agree. David Murphy decided to take on these issues directly at Anderson University: "For me, part of the reason I teach history is to understand why the good and the bad that has been perpetrated or achieved by us has happened. This is supposed to be a Christian institution, so-called, and I'm not part of this denomination. I have no ties to it at all. But I think that if you take the religious and ethical formation tasks of this institution seriously—and I think, since I'm employed by them, it's my responsibility to do so—then the Holocaust course raises questions that these students, mostly young people of faith, need to address. So here it serves specific moral and ethical purposes. I think anywhere it would, but here those are especially relevant. You know, I don't have any illusions about what a couple of years of college education will do. I don't think it will change any of these people's lives, to tell the honest truth. But I hope that in some cases I can start them thinking about questions of tolerance and what the proper relationship of the individual to the state—and responsibility for those around us—is."

Professor David Hackett from the University of Texas in El Paso believes that the Holocaust course speaks to the deeper moral and ethical concerns of students who are hungry for these issues. With a fully secularized school system, they have no opportunity to discuss issues of life and death and the choices one makes as a human being. Hackett uses the context of the course to convey the message that life is the sum of all the choices one makes. It is not made by a single decision, but through an accumulation of ethical issues. Although Hackett is aware that other scholars in the field may feel uncomfortable with his format, he devotes the last segment of his course to "Lessons from the Holocaust," where these kinds of ethical issues are discussed.

From the responses of those who were interviewed, there are more professors who agree with this viewpoint than may be apparent. Katharine Kennedy, professor of German history at Agnes Scott College, says, "I teach about the Holocaust with the hope that students will grapple with fundamental questions about responsibility, racism, anti-Semitism, guilt, faith, victimization, memorialization, and memory." Professor Steven Hochstadt of Bates College believes that the course "provides an opportunity for me and for students to think about certain kinds of moral and ethical issues that inevitably come up in thinking about the Holocaust, and somehow seem a little bit out of place in a normal history course. . . . Issues about racism. When is it all right to resist authority? Questions like that. These are the questions I ask them to discuss in their discussion meetings, and I think it's very valuable to talk about those issues in the Holocaust milieu."

Apparently, it is possible to integrate issues of morality and ethics into the historical context when presenting the facts of the Holocaust. Rebecca Boehling, professor of German history at the University of Maryland, claims that the course she teaches is itself a course about diversity; and according to Professor Joseph Bendersky from Virginia Commonwealth, since American students "have grown up in what is basically a professed climate that leads to diversity, they have trouble grasping that at one point very serious people entertained anti-Semitic ideas, or that racial theories had mainstream adherence." Geoffrey Giles, professor of European history at the University of Florida, believes that the ultimate message of such a course should be the need for tolerance: "I think one of the other important points is how seemingly harmless prejudices grow into something much more serious very easily." He spends considerable time during the early weeks of his course teaching about the roots of anti-Semitism in Europe. Although students complain that they are anxious to move ahead, he notes that "when they've gotten to the end of the course and have a better appreciation, then they realize why it was important to look at that background and to see what a seamless progression there was."

The issue of ethics and morality was directly addressed by all those teaching Holocaust courses at the three military academies. A discussion about the personal responsibility of an officer for his or her ethical conduct even under orders was confronted head-on during classroom discussions. Professor Larry Thompson, at the Naval Academy in Annapolis, explained that the Naval Academy is an institution educating officers who would either make a career of the military or would be likely to continue in some form of public service. "So, one of the reasons I think the course is so valuable, even beyond its ethical implications straight on, is the fact that these students become acutely aware, because I make them that way as they go through the course, that the individuals who planned, participated, and executed [the Holocaust] were all public servants—whether they were civil servants, military, paramilitary, police. We talk about the participation of accountants, lawyers, railroad specialists, transportation specialists, insurance [agents], individuals working for the state from top to bottom. They were public servants. The whole show." With specifically this issue in mind, General Carl Reddel, who was the first to introduce Holocaust studies into the Air Force Academy, felt that the course was a significant part of "the process of developing a new type of public servant."

A particularly dramatic instance of the issue of morality within the context of a Holocaust course was raised by Kees Gispen, professor of history at the University of Mississippi. "I think that one of the things I have done is focus more on the perpetrator side and ask them, Could they do this sort of thing? And I have been astonished that they say yes. They say yes. They are so relativistic. They say if your government tells you to do this, if everybody else around you does it, if it's all culture, you do it too. And so I get all worked up and I say, Would you murder someone? Would you do this or that? Well, they get a little nervous sometimes. And then, by the end of a course like that, they think harder about their own individual responsibility in participating in society and whatever society says and does, and where they should draw the limit, or that they can draw the line and say I don't do that. And that, I think, is actually valuable, but hard to achieve. So it's emotionally very draining. It takes a lot of effort."

THE EMOTIONAL BURDEN ON HOLOCAUST EDUCATORS

The emotional drain and the burden of the course on the lecturer were issues raised by many of those interviewed. As academicians, they had to wrestle constantly with the challenge of presenting the objectively researched material while restraining their own emotional responses to this material. This issue of the conflict between the objective presentation of material and the lecturer's emotions was most powerfully illustrated in a scene described by Professor Daniel Rogers from the University of Southern Alabama: "I have to say that I get really depressed teaching it. I can get right into the middle of that course, and I'm standing up there teaching it like any other subject, and it really gets to me that I'm teaching it like any other subject. . . . And so I stop at that point, and I say to the students that I'm getting really mad because I'm treating this like any other course. I had this sort of visual presentation, because I think they like certain information really made clear to them, like the way people died in the Holocaust. So I had it broken down into a message. And I'm like on point three, part D, and I said it's obscene. I'm up here ticking these things off like I'm teaching you how to fix a clock or something."

Rogers concluded from this incident that after teaching the course five times, it would be necessary for him to take a year off, and then afterward he would return to teach the course biennially. There are many who agree with this solution. "You can't [teach about] vast murder every Monday, Wednesday, and Friday and not have it take a toll," says Arnold Kramer from Texas A&M. "It does take a toll." This is a toll, however, that all those interviewed are willing to pay because they believe that such a crucial event—about which more and more information is becoming available—is an important and worthwhile subject to teach.

THE COURSE FORMAT

Before summarizing this portion on the content of the Holocaust courses now being taught in university campuses around the country, some words should be said about the variations in their formats. These variations range from small discussion seminars to large lectures. Among the different contexts in which the course is offered are senior-level research seminars, freshman electives, and graduate reading courses at the master's and doctoral levels. Professor Robert Krell, a professor of psychiatry in Vancouver, British Columbia, teaches one of the only courses in the world on massive psychic trauma, which he offers in the context of a medical school to senior residents in psychiatry. Since Vancouver has many refugees from Cambodia and South America, Krell, who is himself a child survivor and an expert on the medical abuses of physicians during the Holocaust, has found a way to make the Holocaust relevant to psychiatric residents dealing with current survivors of persecution.

Holocaust courses are taught to students at every academic level from undergraduate freshmen to doctoral candidates. The context in which these courses are taught also varies greatly. Some historians offer the course within the history department and gear it specifically toward upper-level history majors. Many others list the course as an elective in the general humanities curriculum and have students with majors as diverse as engineering and fine arts. Holocaust courses are also frequently cross-listed between several departments such as history and literature, Judaic studies and philosophy, or religion and history. There are even triple listings. The Holocaust course that Leo Spitzer teaches at Dartmouth with his wife, Marian Hirsch, is listed in the history, comparative literature, and Jewish studies course offerings.

With the growing public interest in Holocaust-related issues, several university courses are geared toward outreach to the broader community. David Hackett (University of Texas) teaches a summer workshop on the Holocaust each year for schoolteachers who receive graduate course credit, and Deborah Abowitz (Bucknell University) taught the course for an Elderhostel. Each year since 1984, Ronald Smelser (University of Utah) has held a one-day, for-credit seminar about the Holocaust on Holocaust Memorial Day.

There are also variations in the courses' time formats in terms of how often the classes meet and when. Joseph Bendersky (Virginia Commonwealth) regularly teaches an intersession course, and Jay Baird (Miami University, Ohio) teaches a three-hour discussion seminar one afternoon a week during the spring semester. He then organizes a three-day trip to the United States Holocaust Memorial Museum. With this format he finds that the students have an opportunity to form close bonds and that communication within the class deepens. Several other professors, such as Leo Spitzer (Dartmouth) and Russell Lemmons (Jacksonville State University, Alabama), have also taken their classes to the Holocaust Memorial Museum, but the feeling seems to be that many young Americans have already had an opportunity to see the museum, and it may become less compelling in the future.

Two professors who were interviewed, Dewey Browder (Austin Peay, Tennessee) and Donald McKale (Clemson University), taught their Holocaust classes as a study tour in Europe, where they visited sites that were relevant to the Holocaust. McKale's study tour included short stops in London, Paris, and Berlin, where he and his students viewed former Gestapo headquarters and various exhibits related to the Holocaust. They then went to Krakow in Poland, and to Auschwitz. "That was the most powerful part of the trip," McKale notes. "We spent almost a whole day in Auschwitz. We were given a conducted tour by one of the archivists, museum people there. Very good. And that night we met back in our hotel in Krakow. Our discussion lasted well over two hours, which is pretty remarkable. They had a lot on their minds after they saw Auschwitz."

Although most professors find a preferred format and generally teach their course that way each year, there are some who have had extremely varied experiences. When Doris Bergen taught at the University of Vermont, she had inherited from Raul Hilberg a large lecture class with 120 undergraduates at all levels except freshmen. After moving to Notre Dame, she has taught in many variations, including a discussion class for eighteen freshmen, a graduate-level seminar, a lecture course for sixty-five sophomores, and some summer courses.

What virtually all these courses have in common is the opportunity to show films, slides, and videos, and to raise questions that lead to discussions. Large lectures are divided into discussion groups that meet regularly. For example, Steven Hochstadt, a professor of German history at Bates College in Maine, has had an overflowing class of up to one 150 students every other year since 1992. It is the largest elective course in the college. As Hochstadt notes, "The way all of our history courses are organized at Bates is that if they are bigger than a seminar, we break them up into discussion groups each week. But what was I going to do with 150 students? If I broke them up into discussion groups, I'd be teaching every hour of every day. So that was impossible. But I really felt that just meeting in this enormous group was not enough. So I decided that I would break them up into discussion groups but I wouldn't go. They would have to have their discussions without me. And they would have to do a good job in this."

Hochstadt then described the method he developed for these group discussions. He gives all the groups a topic to discuss with relevant readings on that topic and instructions on questions that should be raised and on how the discussion should be conducted. Each group had to choose a discussion leader who also got some minimal training from Hochstadt, and someone in each group was assigned to write notes about the discussion and hand in a report on it. Hochstadt reads these reports and hands them back with comments. He then added another dimension. Each year he asked for student volunteers from the course who would like to go to the local public schools in Maine and teach for an hour about the Holocaust. There were always at least thirty volunteers who were given a bit of training and then sent off to the local high schools and junior highs. "This year I'm changing that service-learning component. Instead of having it be completely voluntary after my course is over, I'm integrating it into my course. Everyone is going to get the training. The teaching will still be voluntary, but everyone will get the training." Hochstadt is convinced that being forced to think about how they would teach the Holocaust for an hour or two is a very valuable experience for his students.

It is not easy to make a facile summary of how the Holocaust is being taught on college campuses. In response to those critics who question the place of Holocaust studies in an academic setting, it seems that there is little cause for concern. These courses are being taught by dedicated academicians who convey to their students the complexity of the subject while moving ahead toward greater clarity on issues related to many aspects of history and of human behavior. Professor Peter Hayes from Northwestern University points to the importance of these courses. From his study of the German banking system, he saw how easy it was for people to acquiesce in activities that cause unspeakable harm when there is no reason for them not to do so except for a moral one. According to Hayes, if people are to turn away from the path of least resistance, they must have a vocabulary with which to define the situation that confronts them and a vocabulary with which to say no. "That's what these courses do. The courses give them examples of what it means when you don't say 'no,' " Hayes notes.

Hayes continues, "They teach students how real evil doesn't come in the guise, initially, of a monster. We're teaching adolescents, and they think somewhat simply in many cases, as we're all prone to do, that evil is going to be as recognizable as Adolf Hitler's face, and it's not." From his research, Hayes has found that evil can be in the innocuous form of a bank manager who contributed the funds to build a factory while thousands of slave laborers were being worked to death on the site. For that manager there was no risk involved. His superiors were pleased with his contribution, and he was able to make a profit. What you have to do is to show students the way this happens. Yes, it also does happen with blood dripping from its fangs, that's for sure. And you've got to show them that being against hatred is necessary but it's not enough. The banality of evil and all the seductive forms it comes in. You really have got to show them that. Then they learn the vocabulary of saying no. So insofar as we can say what are we doing here, what are we hoping that they will walk away with, I like to think of it in terms of a vocabulary that they will be able to use if they ever have to. It's on the principle that it's hard for us to have thoughts that we can't articulate. We need words in order to have thoughts. They need examples, cases and so forth in order to think that certain things are possible." In response to critics of the place of Holocaust courses in the college curriculum this would seem to be an example of how "learning remains the best antidote to humanity's most inhumane impulses."

The Students

WHEN ZEV WEISS AND THE HOLOCAUST EDUCATIONAL FOUNDATION began their outreach to university campuses in the late 1980s, the goal was to introduce courses on the Holocaust, and in the previous sections the substance of some of these courses was described. The courses have been taught by academics who are either recognized scholars with expertise in this field, academicians from a wide variety of disciplines who have gained sufficient expertise to teach Holocaust studies, or graduate students who are in the process of gaining this expertise. Who, then, are the students attending these courses? Is there anything in particular that can be said to characterize them? What drew them to the course, and what kinds of questions do they ask? And finally, what is the response of students to the Holocaust course once they have taken it?

These questions were posed to the academics who were interviewed. Their answers indicated that a broad profile of young Americans was enrolled in Holocaust courses. Although there were a few universities in the East where up to half the students were Jewish, the vast majority were not. There were campuses like the University of Utah, where most of the students are Mormons, and Pacific Lutheran University, where there are many young Protestants who take their religion very seriously. At the University of Texas in El Paso, most of the students are from Hispanic backgrounds, and in both the University of North Dakota and Austin Peay University in Tennessee, several students told their professors that they had never seen a Jew. In fact, as has been pointed out, the vast majority of both those who are teaching and those who are taking Holocaust courses is not Jewish. In size, the classes range from small seminars of twelve or fifteen students to large lectures with more than 200, and they attract students who are majoring in a wide variety of subjects, including engineering and computer sciences, although most students are from the humanities or social sciences.

Virtually everyone interviewed said that there was a consistently high interest in the course, and most said that registration had to be capped or the class would overflow. This ongoing and universal interest had been largely unanticipated. It would seem to belie the predictions that with mass media overexposure and the accompanying politicization and trivialization of the subject, it would become a fad that would fade. What seems to attract students to this course varies from the prurient to the profound, from an intense interest in the Second World War and the Nazi regime, to an interest in the psychology of human behavior.

The range of student interest is extremely broad, but within most Holocaust courses there are generally enough topics to meet different needs. Individuals are also attracted because of unresolved issues in their personal lives. Several professors spoke of students who were the descendents of German or East European immigrants and who revealed to them that a father or grandfather had been in the German army or among the Ukrainians who may have participated in the slaughter. Assimilated Jewish students have stated that they find themselves feeling closer to their heritage. Other Jewish students are dismayed to learn about the Jewish councils, capos, and police, whose roles have often been labeled collaborative. Some students disclosed that their parents had converted to Christianity in order to escape the persecution.

For students who are observant Christians it is generally a shock to learn about the active role played by the German churches in the extreme anti-Semitism of the period they were studying. Occasionally, an exchange student from Germany or Eastern Europe will reveal extreme discomfort with the facts that are presented. A Holocaust course resonates for each of these students in different ways, and each seeks his or her own way to deal with problems of personal and family identity. Therefore, as the course proceeds, both group dynamics and individual dramas are taking place.

HOLOCAUST DENIERS

Holocaust denial and the reconstruction of history are well-known phenomena. There are certain regions in the United States where it is more prevalent, although university courses on the Holocaust rarely attract students who deny that the Holocaust, or certain aspects of it, took place. David Meier, professor of German history at the University of North Dakota, explains why he has not had any Holocaust deniers in his classes: "Their point of view is going to be that an institution that offers a course on the Holocaust is, by definition, catering to a pro-Jewish, pro-Israeli, pro-Zionist point of view. And in more extreme groups, they are going to link that with the idea that they are covering up the Jewish conspiracy to control the United States, banking, U.S. military, United Nations—take your pick. So they won't even enroll in the class."

Although almost all of those interviewed said that they had never had any Holocaust deniers enrolled in their classes, there were a few dramatic exceptions. Professor Barry Rothaus from the University of Northern Colorado had a student who was a self-confessed Nazi. According to Rothaus, "He would listen to the speeches of Adolf Hitler as he walked from class to class. He had one of these earphone arrangements. And he finally in class said that he was tired of hearing about the suffering of the Jews; there were other people who suffered too; and why don't we set the record straight. He continued on this, and after two or three of these outbursts, I said that I would be happy to talk to him privately about these things after class, because he was disturbing the continuity of the class. The students had complained to me about him. They didn't like what he was saying. He finally dropped the class, but he did everything but put an armband on." Rothaus also had a student whose grandfather had been in the SS. The grandfather had told his grandson that everything he was being taught in class was a bunch of Jewish lies. This student found himself caught between a person whom he loved and the reality of what he was reading and hearing about in class.

Professor Arnold Kramer at Texas A&M was the only one who said that he regularly has at least one Holocaust denier in his class each year. He has decided to handle the situation openly and allow the class members themselves to turn against the student, which they invariably do. Some of these deniers collect Nazi memorabilia, including armbands, daggers, and other items with swastikas on them. When they propose bringing their collections to class, Kramer encourages them to do so. He then explains to the class that these objects are part of the Nazi symbolism, some of the benefits that the

Germans got in exchange for their independence. Although these things have a certain appeal, he asks the class whether they would murder people for the privilege of wearing them. "I try to put it in perspective," Kramer explains. "Yes, you've got an armband, and yes, you've got this and that. But think of the exchange. The ability to wear an armband puts you at the top of that slippery slope that ends in a death camp."

Professor Dagmar Herzog from Michigan State also had a student who was a Nazi fanatic. He knew many facts about SS officers, and there were heated arguments between him and the more concerned Jewish students in the room. When this student questioned the record of Jewish resistance, Herzog had to review what she had taught about the intra-Jewish disputes concerning resistance and the collective punishments that often made individual acts of heroic resistance questionable in the eyes of a community that was unaware of, or unwilling to believe in, the inevitability of its fate. The pro-Nazi student wrote a long testimonial at the end of the class about how much the course had meant to him, but Herzog doubts whether it had any real impact on his views.

Most of those interviewed discuss the phenomenon of Holocaust denial in their course in order to make the students aware of its existence, and some have had students who have brought personal experiences with deniers to class discussions. Other professors, however, believe that the subject of Holocaust denial is not worthy of any kind of attention. They think that the facts are indisputable and that there is too much important material to cover to waste time on the ravings of a fringe group of fanatics. It is their hope that through the course the students will have been supplied with the necessary tools to refute whatever indefensible claims are made by deniers whom they may encounter during their lives.

THE FOCUS OF STUDENTS' INTERESTS AND QUESTIONS

Whatever their backgrounds or major fields of interest, students generally pose certain questions. How could people do this to other people? How could they engage in such behavior? What did the people around them and people in other countries know about what was happening? And why didn't the Jews resist? These are questions that have generally been categorized as relating to the perpetrators, the bystanders, and the victims. One of the methods devised to deal with these questions, as several of the interviewees described, is to ask the students to write three papers on a subject that they have researched during the course using the first person. The students are asked to write a paper from the perspective of a victim, a perpetrator, and a bystander in order to reach a deeper understanding of the complexity involved and to question the easy labels they have heard in the mass media.

Donald Schilling, professor of history at Dennison University, feels that dealing with these questions is an essential element in the course: "I want students to look at the behavior of people who are caught in extraordinarily difficult situations, particularly the victims, and to be able to have some empathy and understanding of why they did what they did and what kind of choices they had. And the choiceless choices they had. I also want them to be aware that it's easy, after the event, to sit in judgment. To say, well, we would have behaved differently. Whatever our role would have been. A bystander, a German. And I want to complicate that for them. Have them recognize that as human beings I guess we have weaknesses. When you look at the perpetrators, that raises questions about our own ability to become perpetrators. It wasn't a uniquely German phenomenon. But as human beings, we have to look carefully at who we are and how we conduct ourselves in our daily lives in light of the Holocaust. I really want students to wrestle with some important moral issues in their own lives and personal issues on a personal level. Not just an investigation into the past, which is removed and abstract."

Students are often fascinated with the person of Hitler and with what could have motivated him to think and behave the way he did. Among the less mature students there is often an attraction to the trappings of fascism, with its goose-stepping leather boots and military salutes. The challenge of confronting student romanticization of these symbols was mentioned by a number of the interviewees, who hope to point out the connection between these outward trappings and the price that is paid for them by the suppression of individual and group freedom.

Most Americans who have grown up in a culture that at a minimum pays lip service to tolerance and diversity find it difficult to grasp the depth of anti-Semitism in Europe not only during World War II, but also for many preceding centuries. Although they are often impatient with the emphasis on anti-Semitism as a background to the events that followed, it is a background to which they later refer when questioning some parts of the unfolding events. As mentioned, many Christian students are shocked to discover the church's contribution to the pervasiveness of anti-Semitism mainly in Europe, but to some extent in the United States as well. In fact, Professor Marvin Swartz at the University of Massachusetts generally asks his Jewish and non-Jewish students whether they have ever witnessed any instances of anti-Semitism in their lives, and there are usually no students in the class who have not witnessed such instances.

In a related issue, perhaps unexpectedly, students expressed an interest in knowing whether their professor was Jewish. This appeared to be a source of greater concern among the non-Jewish teachers, and their responses varied considerably. Rebecca Boehling, professor of history at the University of Maryland, was aware that her students could not figure out whether she was Jewish, and she would have preferred not to address the issue. However, she had a Southern Baptist teaching assistant who asked a question in class that made it essential that she answer that she was Catholic, not Jewish. Other professors let the students know directly that they are not Jewish, perhaps enabling them to become more persuasive role models in their approach to the facts they present.

With regard to questions about religious issues raised by students, Professor James Waller from Whitworth College finds that for many of his students who are devout Christians, it is the first time that they have looked deeply into the question of evil. If they have a belief in God, they begin to question how God could have allowed such suffering to happen to so many innocent people. As sophomores or juniors in college, they find themselves wrestling with this problem, and not all of them come to a satisfactory conclusion. "I think a lot of them end up doing what many theologians have done: just throw their hands up and say that this is a question that's just unanswerable. It's a problem for theodicy. But for others of them, I think it changes the nature of what they perceive of their own spiritual relationship. They come to view God's role in this world differently than perhaps they did when they began the course."

In a different context, at the military academies, as has been seen, questions of morality often lead to discussions about the meaning of orders. Dewey Browder, the professor of history who introduced

Holocaust studies at the Military Academy at West Point in 1993, sees the Holocaust course as an extension of the value system that is systematically built into the life and the studies of the cadets. While he was teaching the course, the situation in the Balkans erupted, and he and his students discussed the role of the military when confronted with ethnic cleansing. It was a discussion that could certainly have a direct relevance for these students who had years of military service ahead of them. Similarly, at the Air Force Academy, Rondall Rice explained that one focus of his course was what he also called the "slippery slope." The students were vitally interested in questions such as, "When do you cross over? And once you go down that road, do you have to keep going?"

The opportunity to discuss these issues of right and wrong conduct is part of the subject's attraction for many students. The search for moral certainty, which finds no outlet for expression in most university classes, intensely engages the interest of students, even when the failings of the Christian church are raised. Kathleen Dugan, professor of theology at the University of San Diego, explains to students that every tradition has its own failings that need to be remedied. Although she finds that this assertion upsets students, they generally are able to understand her point without losing respect for their religions. According to Dugan, choosing to take a course on the Holocaust requires a measure of emotional maturity on the part of students, and she has had at least one student decide to drop the course because she could not endure facing so much suffering and so many questions about the role of the church. However, most thoughtful students who are willing to ask probing questions about their own traditions are ultimately able to come to terms with their religion in a more mature way.

The questions raised by students generally lead to discussions on morality and ethics that are directly relevant to their lives. Questions of tolerance and the responsibility of the individual to the state and to those around them require considerable emotional input. Naturally, both students and professors experience the emotional drain of the course. Professor Boehling found that students sometimes had powerful reactions to the course materials and then either needed to be comforted or to be left alone. Similarly, Jennifer Michaels, a professor of German literature at Grinnell College in Iowa, was told by colleagues whom she met at the Lessons and Legacies Conferences that students may suddenly leave the room: "They say if a student just walks out, don't worry about it. Sometimes things become so overwhelming for some students that they find it very hard to deal with emotionally."

According to Michaels, this kind of emotional involvement has led to greater dedication and commitment on the part of students than she has found in her other courses. Students are willing to devote more time to their readings and course assignments, and they pour considerable energy into papers and oral reports on subjects that they choose to understand in greater depth. Rebecca Wittmann, a graduate student of the Holocaust who works as a teaching assistant at the University of Toronto, finds that dealing with these emotional issues creates a far more serious atmosphere in the classroom than is found in other history courses. Quite a few of the academics interviewed agreed that, particularly in the smaller seminar discussion groups, there is a self-selective process that attracts more serious students who tend to feel emotionally involved in the subject and are interested in grappling with the existential issues that are raised.

Nonetheless, in keeping with the tendency of Americans to seek happy endings, it is often difficult for students to understand the lingering impact of the Holocaust on victims, perpetrators, and bystanders. There is a tendency to feel impatience with long-lasting damage even though it is now well known that survivors of any significant trauma generally live with the impact of that trauma throughout their lives, often passing on the impact to the next generation. There are certainly many Germans, Poles, Ukrainians, and others who either participated in the slaughter or did nothing to intervene, and who have not done any significant soul searching about their role in these events. However, there are also some who have questioned their own activities and those of their fellow countrymen, and the answers they have come up with have changed their lives. Many of those who teach about the Holocaust believe that there are moral lessons to be learned from it precisely because the past does not disappear.

THE IMPACT OF THE COURSE ON STUDENTS

As has been seen, for several decades after World War II ended, the Holocaust was seldom referred to in books, articles, or courses on this period of modern world history. Therefore, the first major challenge Zev Weiss and the Foundation faced was to include Holocaust studies in a university's curriculum. They believed it was important that this significant event not be forgotten. At the time, it was not known whether such a course would have an impact on the students who took it. Now the answer seems clear. Those who have been teaching Holocaust studies on college campuses over the past decade and longer are quite insistent that these courses affect the students who take them—sometimes significantly.

The critics of university Holocaust courses claim that without objective data on this impact, such claims must be viewed with skepticism. As academicians, all of those interviewed agree that this critique is valid. Therefore, their descriptions of the course's positive impact, which were universal, were hedged with qualifications, and many prefaced their observations with the fact that they were largely impressionistic and anecdotal. John Roth, professor of philosophy at Claremont College in California, is convinced that studying the Holocaust can and does change his students in a moral or ethical way. However, although all of liberal arts education is based in some way on making students reassess their values, it is almost impossible to find quantifiable data to show that this has happened. Chaya Roth, a member of both the Board of Directors and the Professional Advisory Board, attempted to address this problem by gathering data from a focus group of students who took the courses of Peter Hayes and Christopher Browning's in 1993. This, however, proved to be far more complex than anticipated, and the long-term study that is required has never been attempted. Nonetheless, virtually every academic interviewed did have the impression that the course on the Holocaust was having a greater impact on their students than were other courses that they were teaching.

As great as such an impact can be on some students, Earl Abramson, chairman of the Board of Directors, believes that a course on the Holocaust will probably not have a positive influence on someone who is already so full of hatred that he is like a professional burglar who is going to break in whether or not the door is locked. For those students who are on the edge, however, such a course may make a difference in their capacity to assume responsibility for their life decisions in a positive way. Since American culture is very sensitive to the notion of individual responsibility and since this notion is such a strong part of American ideology, Professor Kees Gispen has found that students are able to pick up on this element and to struggle with it during the course. He agrees that the concept of individual responsibility is something that can be reinforced in the context of a course on the Holocaust and that this is ultimately a positive contribution in a democratic society.

Probably the most universal impact mentioned was a greater awareness of the complexity of human behavior and its motivations. According to Professor Steven Katz at Boston University, one of the early pioneers in the teaching of Holocaust studies, it makes a tremendous impression on students that normal people were involved in these events: "And it was done in the heart of Europe, so it really challenges all the assumptions about education and culture and Western civilization." Katz has the impression, based on meetings with students sometimes twenty years after they have taken the course, that studying the Holocaust "raises their sensitivity to all sorts of very profound moral and philosophical issues." Students also became more sensitive to the complexity of historical events. Some professors, such as Jeffrey Diefendorf from the University of New Hampshire and Russell Lemmons from Jacksonville State University in Alabama, felt that the course had changed their student's ways of thinking about history itself, not just about the history of the Holocaust. They had become more aware of the myriad perspectives from which such events can be viewed.

There are several tangible responses on the part of students that bear witness to the course's impact—some a source of concern, and some a source of pride. Although this was certainly not one of the course goals, quite a few of those interviewed spoke about students who were having nightmares and problems with sleeping. On the more positive side, there was mention of a heightened general interest about the subject itself on the campuses. A few professors, among them Leo Spitzer (Dartmouth), Doris Bergen (Notre Dame), and Steven Hochstadt (Bates), spoke of how the Holocaust had become a topic of conversation between students in a much wider circle than the class itself. Students had told them that they were regularly involving members of their family and friends in their readings and assignments, so that the impact reached a wider audience than those sitting in the classroom. This heightened interest led some students to commit themselves to further study. Professor Geoffrey Giles

(University of Florida) and Rebecca Wittmann (University of Toronto) were among those who had students motivated to continue in graduate school with the goal of becoming Holocaust scholars, and Professor Kathleen Dugan (University of San Diego) has had students of education who are now teaching about the Holocaust in high schools.

A general impulse to pay more attention to world events was another of the responses noted by those interviewed. Professor Deborah Abowitz from Bucknell University in Pennsylvania found that her students were bringing in examples of news events and making connections with what they had been studying that were clearly appropriate. They were asking questions about what they could do, and they seemed less apathetic and more involved as citizens. This has also been the experience of Professor Jennifer Michaels from Grinnell College in Iowa. Her students say they believe that if more people had protested against Hitler, much of what happened might have been prevented. This has apparently led some of her students, who are mainly from small-town, middle-class, Iowa families, to greater political involvement. The Holocaust course was their first confrontation with evil, and many told her that it changed their lives.

Many of the interviewees spoke of chance meetings with former students who told them how the course had influenced their lives, as well as of letters they have been receiving from students throughout the years. Professor Jeffrey Diefendorf from the University of New Hampshire received a letter from a former student who became a journalist in Moscow because he said he was influenced by the course to learn more about how the Russians had dealt with Stalin's atrocities. Professor Dagmar Herzog from Michigan State got a letter from a former student working with the poor in India, and Doris Bergen heard from a former student working with refugees fleeing to Florida.

Those who taught at all three military academies described responses that were often quite powerful. Professor Larry Thompson from the Naval Academy felt that what the course had done was "to make them confront the fact that their decisions are always going to be fraught with consequences. What seems to be insignificant can become terribly significant."

If this were not sufficient, Lorrie Fenner, who taught at the Air Force Academy, added, "For future military officers, I think it was extremely important for them to see how organs of government can become places of institutionalized racism and brutality. That peer pressure is a very powerful thing. That to do the right thing is often very, very difficult, but is an imperative. So I hope that [the course] impacted their character in such a way that they will become the kind of officers that we need to have in the military, and more important, the kind of citizens that we need in the world." In sum, Thompson, who speaks for many of those who are teaching Holocaust courses both in the military academies and on university campuses around the country, explained, "I mean, I want both an ethical, moral, and professional impact, and I think we've gotten it."

P · A · R · T I · I · I

Holocaust Educational Foundation Projects

THE LESSONS AND LEGACIES INTERNATIONAL CONFERENCES

DURING 1988, WHEN PROFESSOR PETER HAYES (NORTHWESTERN UNI-versity) had already agreed to introduce a course on the Holocaust and Notre Dame was considering introducing a course, Zev's ideas began to leap forward. That spring he met with Hayes and suggested that they organize a conference sponsored by the Holocaust Educational Foundation. From the beginning, the concept was to have a small conference involving real interchange among the very best people in the field, not just a gathering to which many would come but few would really listen to one another. Although neither Zev nor Hayes had ever run an international conference, they decided that it would be important to invite the best-known scholars from the United States, Israel, Europe, and elsewhere around the world who were working on Holocaust-related studies.

Armed with a list of the major scholars in the field, Zev and Hayes set about lining them up for the conference one by one, and had almost no refusals. Raul Hilberg, Saul Friedlander, Yehuda Bauer, James Young, Hans Mommsen, Lawrence Langer, David Vital, Steven Katz, Berel Lang, and Michael Marrus were among the well-known academics who were invited to make presentations in November 1989. Zev and Hayes took care that each of the conference participants would feel well cared for, and they invested considerable time and energy in making suitable arrangements. They arranged for the use of the James L. Allen Center, a beautiful conference facility at Northwestern University, and they filled the conference schedule with plenary sessions, panels, and informal get-togethers. A friend of Zev's who owned a car dealership scheduled a fleet of cars to pick up the participants from the airport. The best food was served at the communal meals. Members of the Foundation's Professional Advisory Board worked hard to make their first conference a success. They took charge of the registration arrangements and helped to get things set up properly. After debating for several weeks about a name for the conference, the Foundation ultimately chose one suggested by Allen Siegel, a member of the Professional Advisory Board: Lessons and Legacies.

The conference (November 11–13, 1989) attracted about 150 participants and was an overwhelming success. Its theme was "The Meaning of the Holocaust in a Changing World." In addition to the opening address by Raul Hilberg, there were three major sessions and four panel discussions. Zev had promised the nineteen major presenters a small honorarium, and he was concerned as to how the money would be raised. Board of Directors member Mort Minkus told him not to worry. This was the answer Zev had been given throughout the years by his devoted board, and the money had always been forthcoming. In the end the conference required the raising of about $70,000. It was the first large project on which Hayes cooperated with Zev and the Board of Directors. The enthusiasm of board members and academics alike was universal.

Since the presentations had been of such high quality, Zev and Peter decided to publish the proceedings as a book, which Hayes edited. It was published in 1991 by Northwestern University Press. The book received considerable recognition and many positive reviews and ultimately won the prestigious Anisfeld-Wolf Book Award in 1992. It has been used widely as a teaching tool and has been reprinted four times.

Howard Stone, the Foundation's treasurer, remembered one disturbing event that took place during the first conference. Several of the sessions had been opened to the public and were well attended by students, faculty, and residents of the surrounding community. At one of these public sessions, when Professor Saul Friedlander spoke, Zev was seated in the front row of the large auditorium. When the lecture was finished, the floor was opened to questions from the audience, and a man in the back stood up and asked a seemingly innocuous question. Friedlander was about to answer when he was advised by Hayes that the question had been instigated by Arthur Butz, the local Holocaust denier. The innocuous question had been asked in order to snare Friedlander in an exchange. The man began to hold forth about how it had been proven from an engineering standpoint that the crematoriums could not have killed so many people.

Zev, who had undergone major heart surgery and was known to everyone as a mild individual who never uttered any kind of profanity, became absolutely enraged. He jumped up and ran down the aisle shouting, "I don't have to take this crap!" Butz and his disciple were removed from the auditorium by Northwestern security personnel. After Zev left the lecture hall, Friedlander curtly but deftly refused to answer so contemptible a challenge, and he received a stirring round of applause from the audience.

The first conference was an encouraging precedent, and the Board of Directors decided to take on the challenge of organizing a conference every other year. This would afford an opportunity for the growing body of academics who were offering courses on the Holocaust to meet with one another, exchange updated information, and provide a network of ongoing support vital for the emerging field of Holocaust studies. With all the ongoing and additional Foundation commitments, it was not until October 24–26, 1992, that Lessons and Legacies II took place, again hosted by Northwestern University but with a change of venue to the Sheraton North Shore Inn located in a nearby suburb. The conference was cochaired by Christopher Browning, Peter Hayes, and Zev Weiss, and the conference committee consisted of Sabra Minkus from the Board of Directors and three members of the Professional Advisory Board: Gitta Fajerstein Walchirk, Sondra Fineberg Kraff, and Elsa Roth. Word of the first success had spread, and registration had to be closed since Zev was interested in maintaining an atmosphere of easy, comfortable interaction, which cannot be sustained when the numbers are too large. According to one board member, this second conference, as well as those that followed, was a sold-out event.

There were approximately three hundred people in attendance at the second conference, which focused on "Teaching the Holocaust." It was another success. The quality of the presentations and discussions met the high standards set by the first Lessons and Legacies. Gerhard Weinberg, Yisrael Gutman, and Raul Hilberg, all distinguished Holocaust historians, were key speakers. Professor Donald

Schilling from Dennison University in Ohio edited the second book, which contained the papers presented at Lessons and Legacies II. Northwestern University published the volume in 1998.

Now that the conferences had proven successful and would be taking place biennially, Hayes and Browning needed to widen the circle of those who would share the burden of academic planning and make it a more collaborative effort. For each of the following conferences they asked a group of between ten and fifteen professors to become involved in developing an appropriate overarching theme, work out a general format, decide on topics for individual panels, and then share the responsibility for coordinating these panels. In this way, those who were experts on a subject assumed responsibility for inviting the best scholars in their own area of expertise. Their common goal was to stimulate discussion among those involved in Holocaust education through exposure to current scholarship and issues. They have successfully attempted to bring to each conference scholars doing important, innovative work in a wide variety of disciplines and from as broad a range of perspectives as possible. Their assumption is that such exposure can help enrich the teaching of the Holocaust by the academics in attendance. According to Professor Alan Steinweis (University of Nebraska), the reason the conferences have been "first-rate academic events" is because "Zev gets the very best people in the country in the field, and he trusts them to put together the conference. So he's working with the best people, and they are exercising their academic judgment."

As e-mail became available for the exchange of ideas, communications between planning committee members became easier. In addition, since the German Studies Association met every autumn, that meeting became a convenient place to get together and work out the plans for the following year's Lessons and Legacies Conference. Over the years, those involved in the planning committee have included Professors Geoffrey Giles (University of Florida), Alan Steinweis (University of Nebraska), Jeffrey Diefendorf (University of New Hampshire), Deborah Abowitz (Bucknell University), Leo Spitzer (Dartmouth), Donald Schilling (Dennison University), Ronald Smelser (University of Utah), Doris Bergen (Notre Dame), Larry Thompson (Annapolis Naval Academy), Omar Bartok (Brown University), Dagmar Herzog (Michigan State), Rebecca Boehling (University of Maryland), Alan Berger (Florida Atlantic), and others.

Although the overall arrangements have been standardized, considerable time and effort are involved in the planning of a conference. Motivation, however, has remained high, and the efforts of committee members are generally sustained through the encouragement and support of Hayes, Browning, Zev, and other colleagues involved in the Foundation's many activities. As Dagmar Herzog (Michigan State), one of the hard-working planning committee members, remarked, "It's just a privilege being with these other scholars. They're all really nice human beings."

Lessons and Legacies III was held at Dartmouth College October 22–24, 1994. Elie Wiesel was the keynote speaker, and the topic was "Memory, Memorialization, and Denial." At this third conference, in addition to the plenary and the panel sessions, another feature was added that was enormously popular with conference participants. This was the teaching workshop. It became a permanent fixture in all future conferences since it answered a pressing need felt by so many of the scholars and academicians who were offering a course on a difficult subject that they themselves had never formally studied. Unlike the conference panels, whose function was to introduce new research, the teaching workshops became the teaching tools of the conference. They focused on how to introduce interesting new materials such as film, media, literature, and contemporary art in the classroom and on psychological approaches to dealing with the material and with the students. There were sessions on how to teach a Holocaust course for the first time, on gender issues in teaching and in the subject matter, and on the integration of interdisciplinary approaches.

One of the aims of these conferences was to encourage as broad an interdisciplinary approach as possible in the teaching of the Holocaust. Therefore, these interactive workshops were organized by scholars from various disciplines such as media (Professor Judith Doneson, St. Louis University) and psychology (Professor Robert Krell, School of Psychiatry, British Columbia Children's Hospital). Since the teaching of Holocaust in academic higher-education settings had clearly become a key function of the Foundation, offering high-level teaching workshops on this subject became a unique and highly valued contribution the Foundation was making to the field. In fact, some of those interviewed felt that their significance warranted more than the two hours allotted them at the conferences.

In addition, a session on the use of film in Holocaust teaching was also added, since quite a few films were then available, and it was important to discuss how to use them effectively with students. Also discussed was the use of photographs or slides so that students could be shown the importance of noticing details, picking out documents that were clearly forgeries, and discovering small nuances with historical significance. The teaching of the Holocaust had become the specialty of the Lessons and Legacies Conference, and those who attended the conferences found their teaching improved from the experience. Hayes was once again the editor of the third Lessons and Legacies volume, which was now becoming a tradition at the Northwestern University Press.

By the time the third conference took place, a feeling of closeness and esprit was beginning to develop among the participants who had remained in contact with one another during the intervening years. Zev, Hayes, and Browning were again the key organizers, in conjunction with Professors Leo Spitzer and Michael Ermarth from Dartmouth. One of their goals was to encourage the feelings of camaraderie that had been developing as well as to ensure that this feeling would be extended to those scholars who were newly entering the field. The summer prior to the Dartmouth conference, forty-five of the participants had been together on a two-week East European Study Seminar to Poland, the Czech Republic, and Germany to visit the various Holocaust sites. This tour is discussed at greater length later, but it served to create an even stronger bond among those present in Hanover, New Hampshire, in October 1994.

For Dartmouth College, an international conference on the Holocaust was a great attraction. Although money, energy, and time were required from administrators, they believed that these resources had been well spent. Many people were able to visit the campus and learn about college programs, and the open sessions were well attended by Dartmouth students. According to one of these students, although many famous speakers had been to Dartmouth that year, including Hillary Clinton and Haiti leader Jean-Bertrand Aristide, "None has had the impact on us that Wiesel and Weiss have had."

Lessons and Legacies IV was held at Notre Dame in November 1996, with the theme of "Religion, Gender, Genocide." An easy rapport had already been established with the history and theology departments and with the university administration, and the Foundation's board members were delighted with the feeling of openness and welcome that they found at this Catholic university. Some Notre Dame faculty participated in the sessions, and students crowded into those sessions that were open. One of these students was apparently so moved by the public presentations that he convinced his father, a wealthy businessman and alumnus of Notre Dame, to contribute a significant sum of money to the university for the continuation of these conferences. Professors Marshall Lee, from Pacific University, and Larry Thompson, from the Naval Academy, were the editors of the volume published from the papers presented at this conference. Both Thompson and Lee (who introduced a second course on the Holocaust while Browning was still teaching there) became involved with the Foundation from an early stage of its outreach to universities.

As with all the previous conferences, when Lessons and Legacies V, on the theme of "Law, Evidence, and Context," was held at Florida Atlantic University in November 1998, one of the greatest frustrations of the organizers was that it was necessary to restrict the number of people who participated. Because of limited space, financial constraints, and the desire to maintain an atmosphere of closeness, not all who wanted to come were able to participate. Although some universities provided stipends for their professors who attended, about 80 percent of the conference costs continued to be underwritten by the Foundation. Professor Ronald Smelser of the University of Utah was asked to edit the volume that would be published from the presentations at Lessons and Legacies V.

Throughout the years, the high level of presentations was zealously preserved, and those who attended found themselves vitally recharged. Praise for the quality and atmosphere at these biennial meetings was virtually universal among the participants who were interviewed, and they have made a unique contribution to Holocaust education.

One of the problems that arose was that some academics from other disciplines felt that it was time for the planning committee to expand beyond the "small group of German historians" who had a tendency to dominate the field. Holding the planning committee's annual planning session when the German Studies Association convened naturally reinforced this tendency. Although there has been a strong emphasis on the interdisciplinary nature of Holocaust studies throughout the years, the issue of territoriality was raised, and several academics had the impression that the Foundation offered greater support to those whose scholarship had focused on German history rather than on fields such as psychology, theology, literature, or sociology. Although several women commented that the initial group was basically "male German historians," later there was a conscious effort to correct this tendency, and more women as well as scholars from other disciplines were included on the planning committees.

Although there is a tendency for some of those involved with the Foundation to believe that the Lessons and Legacies Conferences are the only ones where serious Holocaust research is presented, this is not necessarily the case. Almost all of the professors who have introduced Holocaust studies as a result of contact with the Foundation have other academic identities as historians, political scientists, sociologists, theologians, and so on, and they attend conferences in these other fields on a regular basis. For some of these academics, such as those in German history or in departments of Jewish studies, there are other opportunities to read papers or hear presentations on issues related to the Holocaust and to interact with other Holocaust-related organizations. However, only at the Lessons and Legacies Conferences is there an emphasis on teaching the Holocaust. According to Professor Roger Brooks, a Jewish theologian at Connecticut College who has been actively involved with the Foundation for many years, the Foundation has indeed carved a unique niche as a source of support and enrichment for Holocaust educators in institutions of higher education.

Two other issues that have arisen could be classified as geographical and organizational. One of the West Coast participants expressed a wish that the site of the conferences be moved westward, but this would involve too many costly transportation expenses. However, most of those interviewed enjoyed the fact that the conferences took place in varying locations. The advantage of moving around is that each university site chosen is rewarded with the privilege of a prestigious conference, and awareness of the Holocaust is heightened among faculty and students. According to Hayes, however, the disadvantage of moving around is that organizing the conference becomes more difficult to routinize. The issue of routinization was raised by another interviewee as well. Was there not a need for more formalized paperwork? However, with the Foundation's tradition of easy informality, there is not much interest in considering the introduction of routinized bureaucratic procedures in any of their projects. Both overhead costs and paper work have been kept to a minimum, and the system basically functions smoothly without elaborate procedures. Participants are informed about the dates for each conference well in advance, and individual problems are dealt with on an individual basis.

As mentioned previously with regard to the conferences, the issue of size is also a troublesome one organizationally. When there are more speakers and more participants, it becomes impossible for everyone to attend all the presentations because conflicts in scheduling arise and choices have to be made, often at the expense of something one is reluctant to miss. As Professor Doris Bergen pointed out, the quality of the sessions remains superb, but as the conferences grew larger, she was simply unable to go to all the things she wanted to. There are growing pressures to enlarge the number of presentations; thus far, these have generally been resisted.

The positive comments about the Lessons and Legacies Conferences made by all those interviewed were abundant. They have generally related to the quality of the presentations and discussions, the sense of camaraderie, networking and communication, the cross-fertilization of ideas, and the new teaching concepts that the participants carry home with them. According to Browning, the conferences have been successful because of the high-quality academic papers given and the books that have resulted from the conferences, which make "really good reading." This is due to the "critical mass" of serious scholarship that has made such fine academic presentations possible. In addition, Browning notes that "the spirit has been different from the normal academic conference. People come who have known each other for some time, so it is something of a reunion. Without the conferences and the Foundation, we would probably have published for each other and taught our own courses in our own schools, but we would not have had anything like the network and the connections that we now have."

Unlike many academic conferences where an atmosphere of academic competition prevails, the Lessons and Legacies Conferences have been able to maintain an atmosphere of "camaraderie, interaction, and mutual help," Browning says. Those attending find abundant opportunity for the renewal of acquaintances and friendships, as well as the making of new ones. More experienced teachers share their ideas and their expertise with those who are just beginning, syllabi are exchanged, books recommended, and the usual grandstanding and pretentiousness generally associated with such events does not occur. When describing their feelings about these biennial meetings, the words "warm" and "delightful" occur again and again.

With the best and brightest minds in the field gathered together, the latest research is presented, and ongoing, high-level, heated debates take place both during the more formal sessions and at meals and casual gatherings. An important role that the conferences have served is in making new research available for teaching, ultimately improving the quality of Holocaust courses currently being taught. Since the Holocaust itself is a subject with so many facets, great care has been taken to expose the participants to new information in as many areas as possible by inviting scholars from around the world, particularly Europe and Israel. In the United States, for instance, many of the Holocaust scholars are focused on Germany and on those who were called the perpetrators. Israeli scholars, however, have focused more on the Jewish civilization that was lost and on the victims. By bringing Israeli scholars to these conferences, both sides are exposed to different approaches and to the mix of research that is being done.

Those attending the conferences take home ideas that often have community reverberations as well. For instance, Professor Marjorie Lamberti from Middlebury College in Vermont attended a workshop on current issues relating to the Swiss banks. When she returned to Vermont she invited Madeline Kunin, a former Vermont governor who had served as U.S. ambassador in Switzerland, to work with her in presenting a symposium on the issue of dormant Jewish accounts and Nazi gold in Switzerland. The result was an extremely well-attended symposium open to students, faculty, and the Vermont public. This was only the latest in a series of public presentations that Lamberti arranged after her return from a Lessons and Legacies Conference. Elaborating on the presentations, she added, "I don't want to labor the point, but I think you see that for me it's not merely a passive experience. It's an experience that inspires me and gives me fresh energies and ideas. It's like getting a new blood transfusion every time you go to a conference that's organized by the Holocaust Educational Foundation."

Board members who have attended the conferences have been enthusiastic as well. According to Leonard Berlin, a physician and one of the original members of the Board of Directors, "I, on a personal level, got a lot out of attending this academic endeavor. I learned. It was like going to school and hearing some superb lectures given by some superb professors. So in the narrow sense, I myself was educated, as was my wife. In the broader sense, of course, it was enlightening, refreshing, and satisfying to see the quality of the give and take among the professors who, in turn, were teaching these courses in the schools."

Although the previous quotations reflect the general tone of comments made by those who were interviewed, there was one theme that was repeated most often. The importance of networking and interacting with colleagues and respected scholars was most frequently mentioned. According to Rebecca Witmann, a graduate student who attended the fifth conference in Florida, it offered her a rare opportunity to meet both well-known scholars and newcomers to the field. Unlike some of her contemporaries, who are doing their graduate studies on other historical issues and feel isolated, through this conference she has formed a network of colleagues with whom she corresponds throughout the year. Since teaching the Holocaust is extremely difficult emotionally, the network she has formed gives her the academic and emotional support essential in this field.

A number of the younger academics mentioned that attending the conference gave them the opportunity to meet the scholars who have written the books they were using and that most of these scholars have been willing to remain in touch and to answer questions that might arise. Rondall Rice, who began teaching the Holocaust at the Air Force Academy in Colorado before he completed his doctoral dissertation, said, "For someone of my experience, that's where I get a lot of my information and knowledge. Just knowing these great scholars. Just to be able to talk to them and then bring that back into the classroom and say, 'Here's what he wrote, but I talked to him and here's what he was thinking.'"

Bringing together scholars with different perspectives results in a cross-fertilization that ultimately enriches all of them. The historians learn about relevant sources in literature, philosophy, and art, while those who are not historians learn to place events in their historical context. Horizons are broadened, and ideas are encountered that ultimately improve the courses that students take all over the country. For many of those who attend, these conferences have become the booster shots that keep them going in a difficult and emotionally draining field.

A summarizing comment made by Lamberti reflected the feelings of many who were interviewed: "The Lessons and Legacies Conferences are surely the best I have attended in my professional life in terms of the quality of the dialogue, the searching, and the rigorous quality of the questioning. The search for answers has been so, so impressive." She then added, "Zev is always in the background, but you'll know that he is the motor that is making everything go so smoothly, and making this conference such a worthwhile experience for the people who go there. A lot of time, a lot of effort is required to make that conference run smoothly, and I have deep gratitude for the people who are behind it."

INDIVIDUAL YAD VASHEM STUDY TRIPS, 1988–1995

During the first years of outreach to academics teaching in institutions of higher education, the Holocaust Educational Foundation offered financial support to those who were interested in developing a course on the Holocaust. The financial support could be used in a number of ways that were important in course preparation, and there was considerable flexibility according to the needs of the professor or the university involved. The money was generally used to buy release time from part of the teaching load for course preparation, to buy books on the Holocaust for a university library that lacked adequate funds for such acquisitions, or to buy books specifically needed by the lecturer for his or her course preparations. It could also be used for a trip to the Yad Vashem Holocaust Memorial Center in Jerusalem. Occasionally, the money was needed to fund a research project in a related area that would help the researcher in his course preparations.

The Lessons and Legacies Conferences added valuable new research findings, and a network of helpful colleagues for those teaching Holocaust courses. In a newly emerging field, which was just beginning to attain academic recognition, such networking and mutual exchange of information was invaluable. It became apparent, however, that a systematic, concentrated course of study would help those who were preparing to teach the course to close some of the gaps in their knowledge.

While Zev was still working full-time as educational director of Beth Hillel Academy and expending considerable energy in outreach to new universities, he had little time to consider how to develop an appropriate resource to meet this learning need. When he retired in 1993, he started to sow the seeds of two major projects that ultimately made a significant contribution to his mission. Before the East European Study Seminar and the Institute on Holocaust and Jewish Civilization were launched, the only available alternative was a month of study at Yad Vashem in Jerusalem.

As the original academic pioneer working with the Foundation, Peter Hayes was the first whose trip to Yad Vashem in 1988 was funded by the Foundation. He had finished his book on I. G. Farben and was interested in beginning to research German big business and the Holocaust. During the month he spent in Jerusalem, he was able to prepare for the course he was going to teach on the Holocaust the following fall.

The next trip to be funded was that of Professors Roger Brooks and Robert Wegs from Notre Dame, who were planning to offer a new course that they would teach together. They spent a month in Jerusalem at Yad Vashem during the summer of 1990, followed by a week's trip to Poland. As with Hayes, they were given no agenda, and Zev trusted them to use the time appropriately. Their goal was to produce a course syllabus by the end of the month in Israel. Their days were spent studying at the Memorial Center and talking with Nili Keren, the graduate assistant who had worked with Yehuda Bauer on his important, pathbreaking book on the Holocaust. She made some important suggestions about films they could use, and gradually the course took shape as they discussed the subjects they would present and the responsibility for each subject. By the end of the month, they had prepared a syllabus for the course that they then taught together the following spring.

This was the pattern that was set for the following five years. The Lessons and Legacies Conferences were filling an important role for those who were new to the field by enabling them to feel part of an emerging field of scholarship, but for those who required a more extended period of study, there was, in addition, a course of study at Yad Vashem. During the next few summers, Yad Vashem organized a five-week, six-day-a-week Holocaust course conducted in English.

Among those interviewed who attended these summer courses in Jerusalem were Professors Steven Hochstadt (Bates College), Jay Baird (Miami University, Ohio), Donald McKale (Clemson), David Meier (University of North Dakota), and Barry Rothaus (University of Northern Colorado). They went in different years, between 1993 and 1997, and the course they attended was not specifically for university lecturers. Most of the others attending these courses were high school teachers from the United States, Great Britain, and South Africa, and although the lectures were interesting, they were not pedagogically sophisticated. Each day a different lecturer would be brought in to lecture on his or her subject, and no attempt was made at either integration or discussion.

This was not an ideal situation. Although spending time in Jerusalem with occasional organized tours of Israel had a significant impact for both Jewish and non-Jewish academics, it was clear that a more efficient way had to be found for the Foundation to help university professors in their Holocaust course preparation.

THE INSTITUTE ON HOLOCAUST AND JEWISH CIVILIZATION

By the time Zev retired in 1993, it was becoming apparent that sending professors on an individual basis to Yad Vashem in Jerusalem to fill the gaps in their knowledge was not the most efficient way to help them in their course preparations. Many of those who were either teaching Holocaust courses or planning to do so did not have a sophisticated knowledge of Jewish history and civilization and had little concept of what had been lost with the destruction of European Jewry. Although the experience of Jerusalem was an important one, it seemed clear that organizing an opportunity for systematic study closer to home was a more desirable alternative. The biennial Lessons and Legacies Conferences offered three days of scholarly presentations, networking, and collegial support, but a more formalized, concentrated, and systematic context for learning and discussion was needed. The Foundation-sponsored East European Study Seminar, which is described later, was the first portion of the response that was organized. The second was the establishment of an annual, two-week, intensive institute that would give those academics who were already teaching, or who were planning to teach a Holocaust course, the historical background and a general knowledge of the Jewish experience in Central and Eastern Europe that went further than what Yad Vashem offered.

The idea of establishing an institute percolated slowly for a time, but once it had been formulated—apparently during discussions with the participants on the first East European Seminar—Zev made the decision and acted quickly. The questions of where it was to be held and how it would be organized were kept in reserve until the basic principles behind such an institute were formulated. Zev discussed the idea with Hayes when they returned from the tour, and Hayes was enthusiastic. Within a few months, four principles had evolved: The setting had to be academic; the course had to be intensive; it had to have high academic standards; and finally, the institute would have to be financially self-sustaining, or it would become a continuous drain on the Foundation.

Calling together his loyal Board of Directors, Zev explained what he would like to do. They all felt it was an excellent idea, and they asked him where he was planning to locate such a course. Since a fine academic relationship had already been established with Northwestern University, Zev and Hayes made an appointment with the new University President, Henry Bienen, to discuss the idea. They proposed to Bienen that a permanent institute be established at Northwestern and that Bienen himself serve as chair of the institute that would be created. He immediately agreed, and Zev began the task of raising the funds to ensure continuity and full endowment.

Zev worked together with Hayes, who served as the institute's director. Because Northwestern University was on the quarter system, university facilities were not available until early summer, so it was decided to hold the institute during two weeks in June. The next step, once the time and place had been determined, was to appoint a teaching staff. Christopher Browning, who continued in his long-term role as academic consultant, made helpful suggestions. The decision about whom to invite was directly related to some seeds that had been planted during the first East European Study Seminar in 1994. As the group was traveling, Roger Brooks (Connecticut College) explained to Zev that most of the professors in the group who were not Jewish had never heard of a Talmudic argument and that much of the Jewish civilization that had been destroyed in the East European towns they were visiting was wholly unknown to them. The idea of an institute with an emphasis on Jewish civilization had already occurred to Zev, and he suggested that Brooks teach the group they were traveling with about Judaism. That same evening Brooks gave a talk on an aspect of Jewish religion and history, and the group responded with considerable enthusiasm. It was quite clear to these professors, who were mainly experts on German history, that there was a serious gap in their knowledge about an important aspect of the Holocaust.

Brooks felt deeply that Holocaust studies could not be properly taught at university campuses without including the elements of Jewish culture that either came to an end or were sharply changed by the events surrounding the Holocaust. He urged Zev to create the necessary organization for such learning to take place. It was clear to Zev and Brooks, and then to Hayes and Browning, that learning about Jewish religion, history, and civilization, and about how all that had been lost with the Holocaust impacted world Jewry, would add a great deal to the teaching of Holocaust studies. Once the idea was presented, it was immediately accepted, and in order to highlight this aspect of the program, "Jewish Civilization" was significantly added to the name of the institute that was being created. It was called the Institute on Holocaust and Jewish Civilization and soon became known as the summer institute.

On the assumption that those who would be most likely to need some course of systematic study would be academics with a background in German history who were either teaching or preparing to teach a Holocaust course, Zev and his coplanners decided to offer enrichment courses in various areas. First and foremost, as mentioned, would be courses on the history, religion, culture, and traditions of European Jewry. As full a description as possible had to be provided, within the time available, of the Jewish civilization that had been destroyed after existing for hundreds of years in Eastern and Central Europe. In addition, the participants would be exposed to both literary and video approaches to the teaching of the Holocaust, which could enrich their courses considerably. Permanent faculty members would be invited to teach each year, as well as guest lecturers who could present material on the Second World War or on controversial issues related to the Holocaust. Since those who were being taught were themselves academics, the presentations could be geared toward levels of considerable sophistication. In essence, it was a master class for academics who knew how to study, to teach, and to think historically but were not well acquainted with the material offered. Zev, Hayes, and Browning had no problems recruiting faculty. Most of those asked agreed immediately to teach.

Bureaucratic procedures were avoided, as with all other Foundation projects. No complicated application forms were to be filled out. Those who were interested were simply asked to send a letter explaining why they wanted to attend. These letters, which gave something of the applicant's background, interests, and the reasons for their desire to attend the institute, were then reviewed. When an announcement for the opening of the Institute on Holocaust and Jewish Civilization was made public in the fall of 1995, within two weeks there were more applications than the facilities could hold. That first year many of those who were interested in attending had already been on the East European Study Seminar, where they had become aware of their deficiencies in knowledge about East European Jewry. To avoid turning down some of these loyal academics who had worked with the Foundation for years, it was necessary to accept forty-three for that summer even though officially there was room for only thirty-five. The first session of the institute was overbooked.

In addition, eight of the forty-three who were accepted in 1996 were graduate students working on Holocaust-related dissertations. The stipulation was that each one had to be recommended by his or her dissertation advisor in order for their application to be considered. This policy enabled the Foundation to give support to a new generation of young scholars who would ensure a long-term future for Holocaust studies on university campuses. When Zev first discussed the idea with Hayes, Hayes was concerned that if there were too many graduate students, the institute might appear less attractive to university faculty members. Zev wanted to take ten graduate students, and Hayes five. They compromised with eight. The mix at that ratio worked exceptionally well. Since then, the proportion of graduate students has increased each year. By the year 2000 they formed close to half of those accepted for participation in the institute. Full fellowships were awarded to all those accepted, which included room and board at the Northwestern facilities.

When the institute opened its first instructional program in June 1996, there were professors and doctoral candidates in attendance from universities throughout the United States and Canada.

Hayes was director, and the teaching fellows included Christopher Browning, the well-known Holocaust scholar who had been involved with the Foundation since its early years of academic outreach; Roger Brooks, professor of religion from Connecticut College; Paula Hyman, professor of history from Yale University; Susannah Heschel, then professor of philosophy and Jewish thought at Case Western University; and Rachel Brenner, professor of literature from the University of Wisconsin-Madison. Zev's encouraging and concerned presence was felt in the background, as it had been at each of the Lessons and Legacies Conferences. Together with Hayes and Browning, he managed to sustain the collegial atmosphere and the ease of interaction for both faculty members and academic participants, which was no small achievement.

Both the participants and the faculty represented a diversity of institutions and disciplines, which contributed to the richness of the discussions. Everyone had an interest in the Holocaust and a strong motivation to learn more about it. The attendees were also motivated because they faced the questions of inquiring students. Some of those in attendance had already taught a Holocaust course for a number of years, and others were planning their first course, but all were aware of serious gaps in their knowledge on the subject since they had never studied it systematically.

The course of study itself was both well organized and demanding, with every hour of the day planned, including time for informal gatherings. The institute fellows lived in a comfortable dormitory setting on the Northwestern campus, and meals were eaten communally in order to allow time for informal discussions. It was an opportunity for some of those newly entering the field to interact on a daily basis with some of the leading scholars whose books they had read and were included in their bibliographies. Although it could have been a problematic mix, somehow the combination of leading scholars, seasoned academics, and young graduate students was highly successful that first year. All of those interviewed who had attended either the first institute or any of the later ones spoke with enthusiasm of the warm, congenial, yet professional atmosphere where interesting, challenging ideas were openly shared.

The atmosphere was sustained at that first institute despite the potential problem of a large number of friends who had already shared an intense summer experience two years previously and who could have created feelings of an "in" and an "out" group. No such situation arose, and the atmosphere was one of warm conviviality despite differences in age, professional status, and academic discipline. Over the years, as the proportion of graduate students was gradually increased, it has required more effort to sustain the easy mix of established faculty members and graduate students.

One of the key messages conveyed throughout the two intensive weeks of learning has been the importance of integrating Jewish history into the teaching of Holocaust courses, rather than either ignoring the subject or presenting it separately. At the final debriefing session on the last day, when everyone discussed together what worked best and what did not, most seemed to agree that it would have been helpful to have more of the Jewish religion presentations in the early part of the program since they provided an important background and framework for the material that followed, including the literature of the Holocaust, which has been incorporated into the institute curriculum since the first year. All the institute fellows interviewed agreed that learning about Jewish civilization was a valuable contribution for them in their teaching of Holocaust studies.

Teaching such a sophisticated group was a creative experience for the faculty. According to Brooks, teaching Jewish thought, history, and religion to such a knowledgeable group and compressing it into the few hours available provide a stimulating challenge, which has forced him to constantly reevaluate what is important and what is less so. The exercise has sharpened his teaching in other contexts. Participants are sent suggested bibliographies well in advance, and with the motivation they have, they all read what is recommended. Discussions are lively, deep, and informed. Brooks's goal is for the group to finish the session having mastered a historical structure in which they will be able to place any phenomenon in Judaism. They may not know specifically about that phenomenon, but they will know to what it is connected. He then uses the four categories of myth, ritual, God, and purity to analyze all aspects of modern classical Jewish life. Although most of those attending the institute are not Jewish, sometimes even Jewish professors or graduate students in attendance are not knowledgeable about their traditions. The examples Brooks gives from Jewish and from Christian rituals resonate differently for each group attending.

According to Gerhard Weinberg, a distinguished professor of

German history at the University of North Carolina who was among those invited to teach at the institute, the reason for the project's success is that the focus is a clear one and the program is academically sound and well structured. Faculty and participants all live in a dormitory-like situation where meals are shared, and there is constant informal interaction. The fact that all this takes place during the summer adds considerably to the relaxed atmosphere.

When asked about the institute and about whether participation had contributed to their teaching, virtually all those interviewed who had attended had only superlatives to offer. Professor Jeffrey Diefendorf (University of New Hampshire) found the program "absolutely superb." As a specialist in German history, he lacked much knowledge of Jewish history and culture. Concentrating on European Jewry gave him important insights into an aspect of the course he was teaching that he had neglected. "We were all there in a small setting. There were lots of opportunities for informal discussion both with graduate students that the Foundation brought in, as well as with academics from other disciplines. I thought it was enormously valuable." Many mentioned that they referred often to the notes they took from the institute when preparing their lectures for a Holocaust course.

The presence of graduate students was viewed as a positive element in the program by all those interviewed. They asked stimulating questions and offered the group a feeling of academic continuity that added legitimacy to a newly emerging field still sensitive about scholastic recognition. Professor Deborah Abowitz (Bucknell University) found that "shaping the next generation of teacher-scholars through our discussion and informal dialogues was very enriching. I'm still in touch with one of the graduate students I met that summer—we continue to talk about our teaching, to exchange syllabi and talk about texts for undergraduates." There were even professors, such as Doris Bergen from Notre Dame, who attended the institute together with their own graduate students. For the graduate students themselves, who were taken seriously and treated as equals in all discussions, this was a unique opportunity to interact with the well-known scholars in their chosen field and to form a supportive network for ongoing contacts.

As with the Lessons and Legacies Conferences, one aspect of the institute that participants found invaluable was the networking and informal exchanges that took place between those who attended. Although it could have worked in the opposite way, the dozen or so participants who had been together on the East European Study Seminar and had already formed a close bond served as a magnet that attracted those who were not within that circle. Another contributing factor was that each individual there had different areas of strength. Everyone was an expert on some of the things discussed and a newcomer to other topics. This interdisciplinary aspect can be a humbling experience, but the institute encouraged people to share their knowledge, thus enriching everyone.

Lieutenant Colonel Lorrie Fenner, from the Air Force Academy, explained how it worked for her: "They bring in people from all different disciplines who are students with you, so it really helped broaden my view as well in terms of literature, art, theology, philosophy, other disciplines, as well as created a network of people I can call or e-mail at any time to ask about a new book, a new movie, a new technique in class. The networking is absolutely essential. [The Holocaust] is also a very difficult course to teach because it's so intense, can become so personal, and it's so horrific, that in some ways, being able to keep in touch and do these networking exercises is therapeutic for the instructors who have to face the horror and the brutality of it all, semester after semester. So the Foundation and the network provide a good support system for instructors who present these courses."

In sum, the Institute on Holocaust and Jewish Civilization offered those attending an opportunity to learn from some of the leading experts in the field and to discuss issues related to the Holocaust with others who teach or are planning to teach Holocaust courses. Through the lectures, participants were provided with a background in Jewish history, religion, literature, and civilization, as well as with ways to integrate that background into the general content of their courses. Through their more informal contacts, participants shared teaching techniques and suggestions about which films and books to use. According to Professor Michael Marrus, those who attend the institute, which he called "splendid," meet together with their peers and with high-profile scholars in the field: "It deepens and extends their knowledge and helps make them more sophisticated professionals in the field."

Since many of those attending were relatively new to the field, it was encouraging for them to discover so many others from all over the country who were also involved. By drawing academics from small and large, public and private, secular and religious institutions of higher education, the institute added an element of stability to a newly emerging field that was just discovering its own strength. The institute has been held annually since its inception.

THE EAST EUROPEAN STUDY SEMINAR, 1994 AND 1997

Geoffrey Giles, a professor of German history from the University of Florida in Gainesville, became the unintentional catalyst for the first of the Foundation-sponsored study seminars. Sometime in the fall of 1993, Zev received Giles's name from his growing network of Holocaust scholars and called him to ask whether he would be interested in introducing a course on the Holocaust in his department. For Giles, the call came out of the blue, since he had never heard of Zev or the Holocaust Educational Foundation. Giles responded with enthusiasm, saying that there was considerable interest in that period and that he was not giving it the amount of time it needed in his courses.

When Zev asked what the Foundation could do to help him develop this course, Giles said that he would find it very useful to visit the Holocaust sites in Poland. In his teaching, Giles had found the use of slides a very successful method of holding his students' attention, and he felt that taking some slides in Poland would add a great deal to a course. Like many of his fellow German historians, Giles had been to Dachau and to various sites in Germany related to the Holocaust, but he was sure that his teaching would be greatly enhanced if he could go to the death camps in Poland, which he had never visited.

Zev immediately agreed that it was a good idea, asked when he would like to go, and said he would work out the arrangements. Much to Giles's surprise, Zev called him back within a few weeks asking him whether he would be willing to colead a whole group of professors on such a trip. There were many professors who were interested in participating in a study-seminar tour of East European Holocaust sites, and Giles agreed to make the necessary academic arrangements. His goal was to organize a study tour that would not be tourist oriented. His plan, therefore, was to arrange contacts with museum personnel, librarians, and archivists at various sites in order to learn about the kinds of records that were available for academic research. The group would then hear about the work that was being done and thus lend their support to the East Europeans working at the sites visited.

Prior to this development, the first ones to go on a Foundation-funded study tour of Holocaust sites in Poland had been Professors Roger Brooks and Robert Wegs from Notre Dame. On their return trip after the month they spent together in Yad Vashem during the summer of 1990, they visited Warsaw, Birkenau-Auschwitz, and Krakow. According to Brooks, the slides he made during his first visit that summer, as well as some of the things he jotted in his journal while he stood on the railway built to transport Hungarian Jews, remain important elements in the Holocaust courses he has taught throughout the years. Teaching about the death camps has much greater authenticity when one has actually been there. The camps were much larger than Brooks had imagined, with the foundations of torn-down or destroyed barracks stretching toward the horizon. He was convinced that he could not have conveyed to his students what they were like without having seen these sites himself.

Brooks also personally experienced something that he had heard from Polish Jews who had survived the Holocaust. Even those who did not look at all like the classic stereotype of a Jew said that they had been instantly identified by Poles. This happened to Brooks himself, and he then had a better understanding of how difficult it was for the millions of Polish Jews to escape the fate that awaited them. There was nowhere to hide. The palpable, underlying atmosphere of anti-Semitism that Brooks felt was mentioned later by others who went on the organized tour. Professor Rebecca Boehling (University of Maryland), who was on the second trip, heard a Polish guide say, "The Jews are here," when their group arrived, even though the majority of those in the group, including Boehling herself, were not Jewish. When Wegs and Brooks returned from their trip in 1990, Brooks suggested to Zev that everyone who teaches a Holocaust course should visit these sites in Eastern Europe.

Apparently, there were many who agreed. When Zev called some professors after his talk with Giles, he found considerable enthusiasm for the idea, and forty-five participants traveled to Europe in the summer of 1994. Professor Brooks was one of those who signed up to go on this first Foundation-organized Study Seminar, since he was interested in a more systematic tour with a group of colleagues. He discovered that Zev himself had never been back to the places where he had experienced such suffering when he was twelve and thirteen years old, and where he had lost all the members of his family. Brooks worked hard to convince him that he should join them. During all the intervening years, Zev had rarely spoken about his experiences in the camps, not even to his wife, Alice, or to his children, Daniel and Deborah, who were now young adults. Zev decided to join the group, and Alice persuaded him to include Deborah and Daniel in the group as well. In addition, Gitta Fajerstein Walchirk and Chaya Roth, two sisters who were both members of the Board of Directors and who had been hidden by their parents with non-Jewish families during the war years, also went with their husbands. Among the academics in the group were a few who had been to some camps, such as Professor Karl Schleunes (University of North Carolina) and others who had never been, such as Professor Kees Gispen (University of Mississippi). Although there was some concern about how this diverse group would mix, the academics, the board members, and Zev and his family all had a powerful experience together.

The itinerary was planned; flight reservations were made; a bus was chartered in Poland; and the group went to Warsaw, Plaszow, Majdanek, Krakow, Auschwitz-Birkenau, Prague, Theresienstadt, Sachsenhausen, and Berlin. Having Zev in the group added a particularly strong emotional element to each site visited because he shared some of his experiences with those around him. There was no one in the group who was not deeply moved by his presence and whose perspective was not strongly affected by the short but overwhelming stories he occasionally told.

Generally, Zev would speak each evening at dinner about the itinerary for the next day. When the group was in Krakow, Zev informed them that the next day they would be going to Auschwitz-Birkenau, and that he particularly wanted them to look at a certain barrack that he had heard was still standing. No one knew what the significance of that barrack was until one member of the group asked why that particular one should be seen. When Zev explained that it was the one he had been in, there was absolute silence. Then, the experience of seeing the barracks the next day and standing with Zev on the grounds while he quietly recounted in detail his memories was overpowering. He spoke of how he had miraculously escaped out of a window after he had already been selected for the gas chambers and was waiting in line for the room to be emptied. There were tears streaming down the faces of those who heard him. For his wife and children, hearing these stories was, of course, particularly powerful. The group went to the site where those who had died of disease were buried at Auschwitz and together said the kaddish prayer for the dead, which may have helped to heal a deep wound of over fifty years.

For Gitta Fajerstein Walchirk and her sister, Chaya Roth, the trip was also extremely moving. They were able to find the apartment house where they had lived in Berlin before they were forced to leave right after Kristallnacht. Together with their husbands, they knocked on the door and were invited in by the present tenant. Although they had been young girls at the time, they still were able to recognize the layout and found many things that were familiar. In addition, they were able to find and visit the graves of their relatives in Berlin.

Sharing such personal events with the group had a profound impact on those who were not directly involved. In describing the impact of the tour, Professor Larry Thompson from the Naval Academy said that he knew beforehand that they were embarking on an "odyssey that everyone expected would be painful, but didn't know how deep that pain would be. This was a profound experience for myself and others, in part not because we were scholars, but because there were also people who were not scholars. They were individuals who were friends of the Foundation, and who had relatives that perished at the places where we were. To see their reaction. They knew this was coming, but in a couple of instances they didn't know. Something happened that hit them right in the face that they didn't know. A relative, in a couple of cases a very close relative, had been exterminated there. For someone such as myself, I had a father who served in World War II, and he was in Germany, in Europe. He was in not the first, but the third wave in Normandy, and then he went all the way through. But he came back alive. So I lost no one, thank God, in the conflict. So this is a completely different experience for me than for some of the others, many of whom were younger than I am, who did not even have parents or relatives who experienced World War II."

At each of the sites visited, Professor Giles arranged for an organized tour led by the local museum curator or archive director, who was able to provide a more sophisticated and rigorous commentary. These tours were followed by discussions led by one of the professors who had expertise in that field. Every evening there were historical, religious, and sociopolitical discussions to which all contributed. For those who were already teaching or were planning Holocaust courses, the sense of physical dimensions, and the actual physical predicament faced by those who had been brought to the camps, was an important addition to their teaching. It was clear why escape from a place like Birkenau would have been almost impossible. Seeing with their own eyes would help the professors give more cogent answers to questions often asked by their students, such as the questions about why did those in the camps not try to escape.

The huge size of the death camps was a theme that was repeated by many of those interviewed who had been on the tour. For others, it was the sight of the rooms and rooms of shoes or hair at Auschwitz or Majdanek that was most powerful. According to Professor Deborah Abowitz (Bucknell), "There's something about being there, walking the streets of Warsaw at the Umschlagplatz, seeing what's left of Mila 18, walking through the barracks at Auschwitz-1, and walking the length of the railroad siding into Birkenau that makes a difference. I didn't believe it when others told me this. It's one thing to tell your students how big Auschwitz was, but when you've walked it, you can compare it in an immediate way with the size of places they know. You can describe the sights, the sounds, and the smells from a more personal experience. Trying to describe the smell of rotting leather in the barracks display at Majdanek is almost impossible—but it has such an impact on our students. And the chance to take my own slides of these places and to pull them up side by side with the old black and whites is very powerful. Being able to describe the way the city of Lublin is built up to the wire fence at Majdanek and the way the local kids play at the camp as if it were a park. Or the couple picnicking at Birkenau. Or the German high school students who were playing "Nazi and Jew" in the gas chamber at Sachsenhausen on a field trip. All these things add to what and how I've been able to teach the Holocaust. This trip has profoundly affected me."

Finally, for some it was the concentrated group experience shared by all that was the most significant. The trip was an intense and highly emotional one, and sharing so many hours on a bus, in hotels, and at the sites visited forged a strong bond that was constantly alluded to by those interviewed who had been on this trip. Professor Alan Steinweis (University of Nebraska) described the group's final meeting on the last day of the trip in the Wannsee House in Berlin. Although many of his professional colleagues pride themselves on their "detached objectivity," everyone there let down their guard and shared in the strong group emotions that surfaced. Thompson expanded on this theme: "If you took thirty or so academics, all of whom are individualists, and sometimes eccentrically so, and put them on a bus, and cart them almost anywhere in this world for two weeks, and have most of them still speaking with one another, let alone liking each other, it would have been a pretty long bet in terms of the odds, in my judgment. I was utterly amazed, as everyone else was, how much we enjoyed each other, how much this came to be a real bonding experience."

The first study tour fully met the highest expectations of those who participated, and Giles was then asked to lead a second group when one could be organized. Although many people were interested almost immediately, the second trip did not take place until the summer of 1997. Another board member, Sabra Minkus, together with one of her sons, joined twenty-two academics on this second trip. Professor Michael Marrus, a distinguished Holocaust scholar from the University of Toronto, and philosophy Professor John Roth of Claremont College in California added their considerable expertise to the daily lectures and discussions. Also included were five graduate students who were working on doctoral dissertations related to the Holocaust. The itinerary was similar to the first trip, and the response was, once again, a powerful one. Professor David Murphy (Anderson University), who was on this second tour, found the visit to Treblinka particularly memorable because of the systematic effort that both the Nazis and the postwar Polish government had made to conceal from the surrounding area what had been done to the Jews. An entire artificial forest had been deliberately planted over the site to obscure what had occurred there. Murphy believed that because of this kind of cover-up, the local population could avoid coming to grips with the atrocities that had been committed in their neighborhood.

As with the first trip, Giles found ways to alter the itinerary in order to accommodate those who were interested in visiting sites connected to their family background. The group made a short detour in order to visit the small town in Poland from which Professor Jonathan Goldstein's family had come. There they met an English-speaking schoolteacher with whom Goldstein had corresponded.

The schoolteacher got on the bus and showed them where Gold-stein's grandfather, the local horse dealer, had lived. In addition, Greg Kaplan, a graduate student who was doing his doctoral dissertation on German Jewish veterans of the First World War, discovered some tombstones of Jewish veterans when they visited the Breslau Jewish cemetery. His excitement at the unique inscriptions on the graves was then shared with all the group members, some of whom were inspired to conduct research in related areas. These kinds of experiences helped to personalize the trip, which was again emotionally powerful for all.

For Sabra Minkus, the pleasure of being with a group of scholars who had done so much research in areas related to their visits was par-ticularly memorable. At each site there was someone with expertise to share with the group. The combination of scholars in related fields, graduate students, and board members was very successful, and as with the first tour the group members formed close bonds with one another. Those who had been to these sites for the first time agreed that it added immeasurably to their teaching. According to Professor Dewey Browder from West Point Military Academy, "There's just no substitute for walking the grounds and seeing things with your own eyes."

In fact, the impact of the trip was such that Professor Donald McKale (Clemson University, South Carolina) decided to take his own students regularly on an East European study tour because he felt that such an experience would be valuable for them as well. Katharine Kennedy, professor of history at Agnes Scott College, sum-marized the significance of the study tour for someone newly enter-ing the field: "That experience was invaluable for giving me the knowledge, materials, contacts, sensitivity, and courage that I would need to teach the Holocaust course." A third East European Study Seminar, led by Professor Giles, was planned for the summer of 2001.

P · A · R · T   I · V

Globalization: Outreach to the Former Soviet Union and Western Europe

BY THE EARLY SPRING OF 1997 THERE WERE MORE THAN THREE HUN-dred courses on the Holocaust offered at institutions of higher education throughout the United States and Canada through contact and involvement with the Holocaust Educational Foundation. Only ten years after he began, Zev no longer had to initiate outreach because professors who were already teaching were referring both colleagues and graduate students to the Foundation. Letters arrived almost daily from academics who were willing to introduce a course on the Holocaust but needed help in getting started. There was also a constant stream of letters inquiring about participation in the Institute on Holocaust and Jewish Civilization, the East European Study Seminar, and the Lessons and Legacies Conference. Although keeping up with the projects that had already been launched could have kept a small staff fully occupied, there were still almost no overhead expenditures. Zev continued to work as a full-time volunteer, with the occasional addition of a high school student hired to help with mailings, filing, and e-mail correspondence. As far as members of the Board of Directors were concerned, much more had been accomplished than had ever been anticipated, and it would have been quite sufficient just to continue with what was already functioning. As usual, they underestimated the scope of Zev's vision and the extent of the energy he was willing to expend on the implementation of his ideas.

In the summer of 1996 Zev was invited to Moscow to explore the possibility of opening an Institute on Holocaust and Jewish Civilization for academics in the former Soviet Union. After seventy years of suppression, enforced alienation from their traditions, and stringent isolation from the world, the post-Soviet population was deeply interested in learning about its own religious traditions and about aspects of world history that had been concealed under the Soviet regime. Soviet Jewry was also reconnecting with world Jewry and attempting to relearn its history and traditions. However, the Holocaust had been a subject that was completely unacknowledged throughout the vast Soviet empire, even though a significant percentage of all Jewish Holocaust victims had been killed in areas of the Soviet Union conquered by the Germans. In the many hundreds of colleges and universities throughout the fourteen former Soviet republics, there were virtually no courses offered on the Holocaust, and the subject was unknown.

Zev was asked whether the Foundation would consider the possibility of helping to introduce Holocaust courses at universities in Russia and the adjacent republics. To some degree, the infrastructure for such a project was already in place. Since 1996, an organization called the International Center for the University Teaching of Jewish Civilization (or Sefer) had been mandated by the Russian Academy of Sciences to help introduce courses on Jewish studies, and the Center was in contact with well over a hundred universities that were already offering one or two such courses. There were both Jewish and non-Jewish professors teaching these courses. Through this network, and through the personal contacts of Professor Victor Schneirson from the University of Moscow, it would be possible to bring together scholars from various disciplines and from a huge geographical expanse who would be interested in learning about the Holocaust and about the Jewish civilization that had been destroyed. What was particularly poignant was that unlike in North America, much of the ignorance about Jewish civilization was the result of repressive governmental policies.

Zev was assured that there was considerable motivation to learn about the Holocaust and about Jewish civilization on the part of a number of professors, and it was suggested that he make a visit in the spring of 1997 to assess the possibility of launching such a project. Before considering this new venture, Zev called together his Board of Directors to discuss the matter. He found a good deal more hesitation on the part of the board members than he had previously encountered. Most were concerned about the possible dangers in such a venture, and they were not sure that Zev's health and stamina should be tested this way.

Chairman Earl Abramson summed up another source of concern: "I, for one, was not crazy about him going to Russia. I said, 'Zev, we must be careful we do not outrun our resources. Rommel went into the desert, and look what happened to him.' If we are stretched too thin so that we can't proceed, we will fail. If I had a singular vote, I would not have gone into Russia. I don't think you can outrun your supply lines, and I thought that was what we were doing. But, he made up his mind and I got on the bandwagon with every one else. He was right, and I was wrong."

Zev suggested that the decision be postponed until he visited Moscow to see whether it could be done with reasonable resources. He arrived there early in May 1997. What he discovered was that the motivation of the Russians was high and that it would be possible to rent room and board facilities at a reasonable rate for a two-week institute in one of the decaying mansions around Moscow. Salaries were extremely low, and Zev would be able to hire an academic coordinator who would help to organize the program for only $150 a month. The total cost of a two-week institute was estimated at about $50,000.

A very important logistical contribution was provided by Board member and Foundation attorney Larry Gerber. He made it possible for the Foundation to function smoothly in the Soviet Union. When Zev returned and reported on what he had found, the board agreed that he should go ahead with the plans, and the Institute on Holocaust and Jewish Civilization in Moscow took place in July 1998. The conditions for acceptance to the two-week institute were a commitment from a tenured member of a university faculty and, from that professor's university, a pledge that a Holocaust course be taught every year. The site chosen was called Voronova, a rundown but prestigious resort on the outskirts of Moscow that showed signs of former elegance. It would not have met the standards of most Westerners, but it was quite acceptable to academics from the former Soviet Union, who were grateful for the opportunity to learn about Judaism and the Holocaust in a systematic way. Twenty-seven tenured academics arrived in Moscow from places as far east as Irkutsk, Birobidjan, and Chelyabinsk in the Siberian region and Almaty in

Kazakhstan, to Kiev, St. Petersburg, Brest, and Belarus in the west. Distances are vast, and there were some who traveled through eight time zones in order to attend.

Among the faculty who taught regularly at Northwestern's Institute on Holocaust and Jewish Civilization, Professors Roger Brooks, Steven Katz, and Judith Doneson agreed to teach at the Institute in Moscow. For Brooks it was an interesting experience. He found that the participants had very different backgrounds from those of the North American attendees. Some of them were Jewish and were quite open about the fact that they were pursuing this course of study and of teaching because they were interested in reconnecting with their Jewish heritage. Although most of those attending had what Brooks called "deep pockets of information" based on the five or ten books in their university libraries, which they had actually memorized, there were huge areas where they had never had access to information and therefore knew nothing at all. According to Brooks, "They knew everything about something. And then you move one decimal point either way, and they say, 'Why would I know anything about that? We don't have that in our library,' so to speak." For instance, although some of them had learned a good deal about the Passover seder, they were unable to place it in the framework of the holiday cycle. For all of them, it was exciting to learn about the whole picture systematically, and they were able to make the connections with considerable pleasure.

The two weeks were extremely intense. Since none of the instructors spoke Russian and the English of many participants was weak, a translator was present at all the sessions. This made communication somewhat difficult. Teaching proceeded at half speed, and no one was certain that the translations were adequate to the nuances expressed. Despite these obstacles and challenges, the Russian institute was deemed a success from the point of view of both faculty and participants. As of 1998, there were twenty-seven courses on the Holocaust taught in universities throughout the former Soviet Union, where there were none before the Foundation's outreach. For a small organization with several major ongoing projects to coordinate and support, the venture took courage and commitment. These are certainly qualities that Zev and the Foundation's board have demonstrated in great abundance throughout the years of their activities.

The next step, which might have previously been considered difficult, was taken in Western Europe. Zev and Peter Hayes made a trip to London in the fall of 1999. They began negotiations with three major institutions—Royal Holloway College, the University of London, and Southampton University—in order to establish an Institute on Holocaust and Jewish Civilization for Western Europe. There were some widely recognized Judaica and Holocaust scholars in Great Britain who could serve as faculty members. After this third institute has been established, perhaps Zev will launch another global venture. Although it is difficult to imagine that yet another such project could be undertaken, neither the Board of Directors nor anyone who has been in long-term contact with Zev and his vision can think that the European institute will be his last global initiative.

The Power of Individual Initiative

ALTHOUGH IT IS CLEAR THAT THE HOLOCAUST EDUCATIONAL FOUN-
dation would not exist without the strong and loyal support of
the board members, it is equally clear that Zev Weiss has provided a
unique kind of leadership. Without it, none of the projects undertaken by the Foundation would have been created. Since Zev's rare
combination of qualities is not always apparent at first contact, one
of the questions asked of all the academics interviewed was their im-
pressions of Zev when they first met him. It would be impossible to
do justice to the wealth of spontaneous outpourings in response to
this query, and any summary of these responses to the many facets of
Zev's complex personality and leadership is somehow inadequate.

Probably the words most often used were dedicated, sincere,
unassuming, serious, modest, genuine, warm, generous, giving, supportive, and helpful. As Lee Wyatt (West Point) said, Zev is "a gentleman in both senses of the word. He is a gentle man, and a gentleman,
and that's a compliment I would rarely give out to people." There
were also words such as otherworldly and mystical, as well as stub-
born, reserved, unapproachable, intimidating, and abrupt. Zev is a
man with a mission who conveys that sense of commitment to everyone he meets. As Rondall Rice (Air Force Academy) put it, "After
everything he's been through in his life, he's worried about the out-
come, and he's not worried about what anybody thinks about him."

There were some, such as Jeffrey Diefendorf (University of New
Hampshire), who were surprised at how informal and low-key Zev is:
"Unlike some survivors who have been involved in Holocaust education, he doesn't wear this as a sort of personal burden that he is carrying to everyone. He almost never talks about his own personal

experience. He is a very modest man in that way." David Meier (University of North Dakota) described these traits from a different angle. He said that Zev is "caring—he's concerned with the individual, he wants you to develop your own potential in a way that you are comfortable with. He at no point either pushes his agenda, or his background, or his involvement." Steven Hochstadt (Bates College) explained, "His power, for me, did not come from my knowledge of what he'd been through. It was from the seriousness of purpose—his sureness that he was doing something important." "I think he shows real human concern for each individual he deals with. It's not like a big bureaucratic organization where you're dealing with some top-heavy bureaucracy. This is not a program administered from afar," noted David Hackett (University of Texas).

Many responses reflected the dual sides of Zev's leadership: businesslike and pragmatic in some contexts, but warm and supportive in others. In Chaya Roth's words, "He is dogged and persistent, and also not particularly heavy-handed." To some who first met him, Zev appeared frail. Larry Thompson (Naval Academy) expressed concern for his physical capacity: "And you worry. He does not look like he's the strongest individual in the world. This individual has really involved himself in a Herculean effort, and you hope that his stamina will hold up, that he won't kill himself in putting this thing together. But as I got to know him, he's one tough guy. He really is, and one determined guy." Ron Smelser (University of Utah) described a different aspect of this duality. He found Zev "quietly soft spoken, but very strong willed." This combination of characteristics is immediately apparent to students when Zev is invited to speak at class forums around the country. The image was often repeated that in a large lecture hall, with poor acoustics, Zev would speak softly, often forgetting to use the microphone, and the students would sit absolutely silent, straining to hear every word. Several of the professors mentioned that in the student evaluations they received, Zev's presentation was noted as the most memorable portion of the course.

Although academic life on college campuses is generally considered to be scholarly and almost pastoral, the world of academia is as fraught with political agendas as are other arenas where such maneuvering might be more expected. Zev's entry into this world with a single-minded mission was not without its complexities. What many of those he contacted found disarming, however, was his absolute trust in their professional judgment and his lack of any agenda other than the introduction of a Holocaust course.

Donald Schilling from Dennison University, who first noted that Zev physically resembled Elie Wiesel and that his gauntness fit the image he had of a survivor, continued, "But then, what began to come across is that here is a man of great integrity and honesty. Truly committed to the advancing of understanding of the Holocaust in ways that are liberating and not restrictive. That is, what immediately impressed me about Zev was the lack of a well-defined agenda. He trusted my professional judgment as a historian as to what should be done, and what kind of course I should teach. There was no effort to prescribe a set of readings or topics or anything else to go into that course. I was given a totally free hand. He just asks, 'We want to help you do what you can do best in the teaching of the Holocaust course.' And that struck me as extraordinary—in an area where there can easily be political battles fought, where it can easily become very politicized. That impressed me. I got a sense that here's a man I can trust. Here's a man who is obviously deeply committed." In a similar vein, a number of professors noted that although Zev never asks whether they have done what they committed themselves to do, they just do it for him because he trusts them to do so.

Zev is very clearly central to the Foundation, yet he seems to have no need to thrust himself into the limelight. "He is a facilitator who emphasizes his place in the background" noted David Meier (University of North Dakota). James Waller (Whitmore College) explained, "He's just so accommodating. So empowering. You don't get a sense, like with some foundations, that the lead person can be kind of obstructionist—somebody you have to get through to try and get to something that will help you. Zev is just so unassuming, accommodating, so willing to take a backseat. He's one of the few people I know who have no ego involvement to them. That's been one of the best things for me about working with the Foundation, getting to know Zev." Michael Marrus (University of Toronto) stated, "Zev has the ability to get people to go to work for him and to do so willingly and eagerly. And I've always thought that this was one of the real attributes of leadership."

The loyalty that Zev inspires is awesome, particularly among the Foundation's board members, who have been devoted to him for decades. "I think most everyone would gladly give his life for Zev Weiss," declared Barry Rothaus (University of Northern Colorado). Those who work closely with Zev are aware of his stubbornness, and that in some ways he is not an easy person to work with, but his commitment to the goals he sets and his ability to execute these goals are remarkable. This is true even though Zev's ability to speak concisely is not always his strong point. Howard Stone admitted that Zev's capacity to implement his ideas did not seem congruent with the way he expresses himself: "Sometimes at a meeting you want to say, 'Zev, get to the point.' For any business to be successful, the message has to be concise, and you have to be able to rattle off what are the important sound bites, or else it's not going to work. Well Zev proved me wrong. I'm wrong."

So what is the secret to his success? According to Peter Hayes, who has worked closely with Zev for more than a decade, "The marvelous thing is that Zev's genius was to set himself very specific goals, and they were never too big or too small. Each of these things has gone that way. Something that was in principle within reach, though at the moment just out of reach. That was the way he did it. And when you look at how successful he was, [it was] on relatively little investment, as these things go. He sets these very clear goals. 'Okay, let's try and get people teaching.' 'All right, let's take them to Europe. Let them see.' 'All right, let's bring them to Northwestern, and they need to learn something about Jews.' And each time it's a slightly different take on what had to be done, but a manageable one. So that was his genius. And it's been a model for the ratio between input and output." As Steven Katz (Boston University) summarized, "I think he's remarkable. It shows the power of will. Here's a person who took upon himself, to create without doubt, I think everyone would agree, the most successful, interesting, high-level program of university adult education [the Institute on Holocaust and Jewish Civilization] for young academics and so on all over the world. It's quite remarkable."

Earl Abramson, the chairman of the Board of Directors who brought Zev to Chicago and has been a close friend to him ever since, was asked what he was most proud of in all his involvement with the Holocaust Educational Foundation. His immediate, unhesitating reply was "Zev being part of my life. I am very proud of that. He is truly one of life's amazing people and performers. Dedicated and sincere. He is a very special person."

Zev displayed his unusual combination of qualities during the compiling of this history of the Holocaust Educational Foundation. When one of the board members made a contribution that was specifically earmarked for the documentation of Zev's remarkable achievements, Zev was strongly opposed to using Foundation funds in this way. He was, however, willing to use the contribution for a documentation of the Foundation's contribution to Holocaust education at university campuses, so the work was begun. What became clear, however, through collection of the relevant information, was that Zev himself stands out strongly as a central component in this process. It would have been quite impossible to document this development without paying tribute to Zev Weiss and to his achievements.

Contributions of the Holocaust Educational Foundation

FIFTY YEARS AFTER THE HOLOCAUST DEVASTATED EUROPEAN JEWRY, the Western world had come to recognize the significance of this event. The careful, competent work of historians was continuing to uncover information about the Holocaust after decades of general silence, avoidance, and minimization. Although an entire generation that had witnessed the Holocaust as victims, bystanders, or perpetrators was aging and dying, written and oral records of much that had occurred were now accessible to scholars and to the general public. Zev Weiss and the Holocaust Educational Foundation have made a significant contribution to both the compilation of these records and to the recognition that has been attained.

The Holocaust Educational Foundation is the only organization in North America working to promote and preserve an awareness of the Holocaust through university education. The United States Holocaust Memorial Museum with its vast resources now plays a significant role in heightening general public awareness of the Holocaust. There are, however, dozens of local organizations that have established Holocaust memorials ranging from rooms within a community center to large local museums. Some of these organizations sponsor seminars for elementary and high school teachers. In addition, there are quite a few dedicated survivors who offer presentations in schools and community centers around the country. There are academic associations that sometimes offer forums for presentations on the Holocaust at their conferences—for example, the German Studies Association, the American Academy of Religion, the American Historical Association, and the Association of Jewish Studies. Each of these organizations publishes a journal that sometimes includes articles on various historical, theological, or religious aspects of the Holocaust. Many of the academics who are involved with the Foundation are also members of one or more of these associations.

What then is the contribution of the Holocaust Educational Foundation? The niche in which the Foundation makes its unique contribution is in the teaching of Holocaust studies in institutions of higher education around the world. No other organization reaches out to the less-central regions in North America and around the world to encourage the teaching of Holocaust courses on both large and small college campuses. Christopher Browning has pointed out, "If you really want to affect Holocaust consciousness in the United States, you have to get into the undergraduate curriculum. That is where consciousness, awareness of educated people in the United States, is shaped. It isn't by building a statue or a monument or a museum. And that was Zev's brainstorm. Really altering the terrain of American higher education. . . . And for an individual, that's extraordinary."

Another significant contribution has been the various Foundation-sponsored activities that have developed to support the growth of Holocaust education. No other organization offers an intensive course of study on Jewish civilization for those who teach university courses on the Holocaust. The Institute on Holocaust and Jewish Civilization brings graduate students and faculty together on an equal basis and creates an academic and social environment in which they work together. No other organization sponsors study seminars to Eastern Europe for academics and holds conferences on the teaching of the Holocaust in universities. It is generally acknowledged that the Lessons and Legacies Conferences are the premiere conferences in this field. Through these contributions, the Foundation has helped to raise the quality of Holocaust scholarship and to attract promising new teachers to the field.

These young academics are then introduced into a warm, supportive network of scholars who help one another with syllabi, bibliographies, and film recommendations, as well as with advice in dealing with the academic and emotional issues that arise. Such support is particularly essential in a newly emerging academic field where the early pioneers had to educate themselves, and where no such courses existed when they began to teach. Their welcome of newcomers into the field is generally genuine, and the Foundation has provided the context in which this scholastic esprit can develop.

Thanks to the efforts of the Foundation, there are tens of thousands of young people in institutions of higher education around the world who are learning about the Holocaust from dedicated, responsible academics. Through the Foundation, these academics have opportunities plus the support they need to update their knowledge on a regular basis and to keep the flow of information in their courses stimulating, interdisciplinary, and pertinent. In addition, through the inclusion of an ever-increasing percentage of graduate students in the Foundation's various projects, the continuity of Holocaust courses on the campuses has been effectively assured. These graduate students are highly motivated to teach a course on the Holocaust at any university where they will work during their academic careers.

A major part of the Foundation's contribution has been its active program of outreach to academics. Through these contacts, Zev has tapped into and unleashed great quantities of hidden potential. Zev and the Holocaust Educational Foundation are an important part of the general growth in Holocaust education as already demonstrated. Steven Hochstadt (Bates College) pointed out that "there'd be more Holocaust education now than twenty years ago even if Zev didn't do this work, but he is a catalyst to encourage people like me, who were kind of on the fence. Give them a little shove over, and there is Zev with encouragement. So I think he's been right there at the forefront of a process that's a bigger process than him. It's a process that's happening. But he's moving it along, encouraging it, providing materials and help for people who are doing it. I think if you're looking for individuals who've had a major impact on the teaching of the Holocaust in the United States, Zev Weiss is one of them. And he's doing it all over the world. The scale of what he's accomplished is staggering."

From the statements of many who were interviewed, contact with Zev and with the Foundation has dramatically changed their lives, and through his quiet encouragement of these dedicated academics, the field has continued to grow steadily. Quite a few of those interviewed have stated unequivocally that they would not be teaching Holocaust courses without Zev's outreach. And others claim that they are better teachers, with a greater depth of knowledge and of feeling, than they would have been without their contact with the Foundation.

Plans for the Future

THE ACHIEVEMENTS OF THE HOLOCAUST EDUCATIONAL FOUNDATION began to surpass the expectations of its board members already during the early years, when they were solely engaged in videotaping testimonies of Holocaust survivors. Since then, the sense of wonder at Zev's capacity to work and to accomplish the goals that he has set grows continuously. At each stage, the Board members have told Zev that what has been done is sufficient and that the next step is probably not attainable. And each time they have readily admitted that they were wrong.

When they are asked about plans for the future, most Board members shrug their shoulders and say that as long as Zev has energy to work, the vision for the future is in his hands. However, they are all aware of the fact that the years have been passing and that no human being is capable of continuing at such a pace indefinitely. Virtually every person who has worked closely with Zev, whether on the Board of Directors or in academia, is concerned about what will happen to the work of the Foundation when Zev no longer has the energy to continue. In the meantime, Zev has been urged at the least to find some help in the office and with the administrative work involved in the Foundation's many projects. There can be no substitute for Zev, with his unique experiences and personal qualities. His passion and dedication are clearly irreplaceable. Nonetheless, neither Zev himself nor anyone else wants the work of the Foundation to cease. Therefore, difficult as it will be to find a suitable helper, all agree that this is the next step to be taken.

And what are the tasks still ahead for Zev and a possible assistant? Among the board members interviewed, there was a general consensus that the path that has been chosen until now should continue to be followed. According to board member Leonard Berlin, "I suppose theoretically the goal is to get every single university in the world to teach the Holocaust. Well, that's not a practical goal. But, nevertheless, I think the goal is to continually increase the number of institutions of higher learning. So that's an ongoing effort. Hopefully we will continue indefinitely." Therefore, as long as there are universities where Holocaust studies are not yet taught, the Foundation will seek them out and provide assistance for establishing a course on the Holocaust and will respond positively to professors and universities initiating contact. New applications for assistance will continue to be considered for acceptance to the Institute on Holocaust and Jewish Civilization, the next Lessons and Legacies Conference, or the East European Study Seminar.

There is no apparent reason why this work should be disrupted. A momentum has been achieved that can continue with appropriate administrative coordination. Zev and Peter Hayes have established the process for new applications, and the three large projects—the Lessons and Legacies Conferences, the Institute on Holocaust and Jewish Civilization, and the East European Study Seminar—have attained a degree of administrative routine that will allow for the incorporation of a new assistant. Board member Leonard Berlin continued, "It will never be the same. I guess it's the same in any business or organization. You have the founder, and then you have those that follow. And I would say that attributes of the founder are a lot different than what you look for in a successor. Because in certain respects, you are not starting from baseline zero. You are looking for maintenance—to keep it going at least at its present level."

In addition to maintenance, those interviewed mentioned some suggestions for possible future development. Alan Steinweis (University of Nebraska) spoke of the fact that no academic Holocaust studies association has yet been established, and that this might be a possible project to take on, with accompanying dues that could sustain it, elected officers, and a newsletter with updated relevant information. The Foundation did have a subsidized newsletter for laypeople that was sent out twice a year between 1994 and 1996. David Murphy (Anderson University) suggested developing a quarterly scholarly publication of research and events, and there were some academics, including Christopher Browning and Peter Hayes, who would like to see more support of graduate student research. Two fellowship competitions, one for current faculty and one for graduate students completing dissertations, would give a significant boost to the field. Although the United States Holocaust Memorial Museum is currently offering research fellowships, they are tied to a residency at the museum, and there is a need for research awards that are more flexible with regard to residence. As with all the previous projects, Zev basically concurs with this need. He is just beginning to explore the idea of creating a Holocaust Research Institute at Northwestern University in conjunction with the Theodore Zev Weiss Holocaust Educational Foundation Chair that has been established.

Roger Brooks (Connecticut College) and Michael Marrus (University of Toronto) suggested that some bridge building between the Foundation and the various organizations in the Holocaust field might be helpful for coordinating projects and sharing information. Such bridging, though not necessarily expensive, is labor intensive, requiring time, motivation, and energy. There are also the challenges of the Internet and CD-ROM applications, which will require connections with technologically oriented organizations. And another labor-intensive project mentioned by several people, including General Carl Reddel, was follow-up research to study the impact of Holocaust courses on students.

Both Ronald Smelser (University of Utah) and David Hackett (University of Texas) suggested that a forum be developed within the Institute on Holocaust and Jewish Civilization for preparing high school teachers to include Jewish civilization in their lessons on the Holocaust. Geoffrey Giles recommended courses on Polish and Yiddish so that scholars can begin to explore the Holocaust archives that have recently been made available in Poland and specifically in Warsaw. Kees Gispen (University of Mississippi) and Dagmar Herzog (Michigan State), who like most of those involved are European specialists, hope to get some help from the Foundation in educating academics about comparative genocide in other parts of the world. Nonetheless, despite these various suggestions, most of those who are involved with the Foundation would be very pleased just to see that everything that has been done until now could be maintained and nurtured, and quite a few agreed with Jay Baird (Miami University, Ohio), who said, "I think it's on a wonderful course now. I wouldn't change a thing."

Zev has always believed in a hands-on approach, and he has been in touch, personally, with all those who have been involved with the Foundation. The organization has thrived on this personal touch, and it has been a source of great satisfaction to Zev and to the professors. No one can do this as well as Zev, and no one wants him to stop as long as he is able to continue. However, as in all human relationships, continuity can be helped along through the smooth transition of a personal introduction. According to Peter Hayes, for the sake of that continuity, Zev "needs to begin training someone who could succeed him. This is such a tough role to fill that it's hard to find anybody who looks big enough for it. But that's the challenge of the immediate future. To reduce the amount of time and energy required to do what we are doing well, and to concentrate on the new things and the succession. And making sure that the connections that exist will continue to exist in the future."

Sustaining these connections is an important aspect of the Foundation's achievements. Peter Hayes continues, "There's a certain esprit to the whole thing. Academia is not well designed from the point of view of motivating people. . . . The reward structure is not set up to make people bushy tailed and so forth. Or perhaps I should say that the range of rewards is limited. And so psychic rewards are very important: connections, friendships, and the sense of being in a common and valuable enterprise. Especially because academia can be atomizing, all of that is very valuable, and we need to have somebody to sustain it."

Transitions go more smoothly when there is a stamp of approval. Zev's paternal presence has enabled the Foundation to thrive. His stamp of approval is important for continuity. Board member Jon Mills sums up the dilemma: "It depends on what Zev wants. None of this matters except what Zev wants because Zev is the essence of this Foundation, and what would he like? It's very hard to turn control over and see somebody do it worse than you. And I guarantee that if he got Mother Theresa, she would do it worse than he. But, a few things—despite what Zev likes or what I like with my company— the kids do better than we. So trust me, this new person will do something better. And you know, it'll change. What can I tell you?"

Zev Weiss, with the support of his small group of dedicated Board members, is a model of quiet, efficient, and highly effective initiative. Without Peter Hayes, Christopher Browning, and all the hundreds of academics who have become part of this initiative, how-

ever, Zev's vision could not have been achieved. The fact that Holocaust education on college campuses is a major attraction drawing
thousands of students each year and enabling them to reflect intelli-
gently on the responsibility we have toward our fellow human beings
is a tribute to all of those involved. Holocaust education is a difficult
subject that is worthy of profound reflection. From what has been
summarized here, it is clear that the men and women who are working with Zev Weiss, either on the Board of Directors or in the classroom, are achieving this goal and deserve much credit for what they
have accomplished.

Appendix A:
Holocaust Educational Foundation
Board Members

Theodore Z. Weiss, President
Earl. B. Abramson, Chairman of the Board
Howard L. Stone, Treasurer
Lawrence Gerber, Counsel
Prof. Peter Hayes, Academic Consultant
Prof. Christopher Browning, Academic Consultant
Dr. Leonard Berlin
Paul Krouse
Judd Malkin
Jon Mills
Sabra Minkus
Dr. Chaya Roth
Theodore Spak
Robert Stempel
Richard Weinberg

Appendix B:
Academics and Board Members Interviewed

ACADEMICS

Abowitz, Deborah	Bucknell College, Pennsylvania
Baird, Jay	Miami University, Ohio
Bendersky, Joseph	Virginia Commonwealth University
Bergen, Doris	Notre Dame University, Indiana
Boehling, Rebecca	University of Maryland, Baltimore
Brooks, Roger	Connecticut College
Browder, Dewey	Austin Peay State University, Tennessee
Browning, Christopher	University of North Carolina, Chapel Hill
Cogan, Nathan	Portland State University, Oregon
Diefendorf, Jeffrey	University of New Hampshire
Dugan, Kathleen	University of San Diego, California
Fenner, Lorrie	Air Force Academy, Colorado
Giles, Geoffrey	University of Florida, Gainesville
Gispen, Kees	University of Mississippi
Grill, Jonpeter Horst	Mississippi State University
Hackett, David	University of Texas, El Paso
Hayes, Peter	Northwestern University, Illinois
Herzog, Dagmar	Michigan State University
Hochstadt, Steven	Bates College, Maine
Katz, Steven	Boston University, Massachusetts
Kennedy, Katharine	Agnes Scott College, Georgia
Kramer, Arnold	Texas A&M, College Station
Krell, Robert	British Columbia Children's Hospital, Vancouver, Canada
Lamberti, Marjorie	Middlebury College, Vermont
Lemmons, Russel	Jacksonville State University, Alabama
Marrus, Michael	University of Toronto, Ontario, Canada

McKale, Donald	Clemson University, South Carolina
Meier, David	University of North Dakota
Michaels, Jennifer	Grinnell College, Iowa
Murphy, David	Anderson University, Indiana
Reddel, Carl	United States Air Force Academy, Colorado
Rice, Rondall	United States Air Force Academy, Colorado
Rogers, Daniel	University of South Alabama
Roth, John	Claremont College, California
Rothaus, Barry	University of Northern Colorado
Schilling, Donald	Dennison University, Ohio
Schleunes, Karl	University of North Carolina, Greensboro
Smelser, Ronald	University of Utah
Spitzer, Leo	Dartmouth College, New Hampshire
Steinweis, Alan	University of Nebraska, Lincoln
Swartz, Marvin	University of Massachusetts, Amherst
Thompson, Larry	United States Naval Academy, Annapolis
Waller, James	Whitworth College, Washington
Weinberg, Gerhard	University of North Carolina, Chapel Hill
Wittmann, Rebecca	University of Toronto, Ontario, Canada
Wyatt, Lee	United States Military Academy, West Point

BOARD MEMBERS

Appendix C:
The Institute on Holocaust
and Jewish Civilization

INSTITUTE FACULTY (1996–2000)

Peter Hayes, Director
Rachel Brenner
Roger Brooks
Christopher Browning
John Efron
Susannah Heschel
Sara Horowitz
Paula Hyman

Steven Katz
S. Lillian Kremer
Stuart Liebman
John Roth
Karl Schleunes
Gerhard Weinberg
Robert Weinberg
Steven Zipperstein

FELLOWS (PROFESSORS) (1996–2002)

John Abbott
Deborah Abowitz
Monica Adamczyk-Garbowska
Michael Allen
John Arnold
Karl Bahm
Jay Baird
Anni Baker
Doris Bergen
Jack Bielasiak
Joseph Biesinger
Richard Block
Rebecca Boehling
Peter Boehm

Wayne Bowen
Rennie Brantz
Arthur Brenner
Dewey Browder
George Browder
Iris Bruce
Gisela Brude-Firnau
Lynn Bryce
Scott Bryce
Joshua Charlson
Joanne Cho
Simone Clark
Nathan Cogan
Julie Colish

Timothy Crawford
Chet DeFonso
Jeffrey Diefendorf
William Donahue
Kathelin Dugan
Henry Eaton
Sam Edelman
Judith Fair-Podlipnik
Allan Fenigstein
Lorrie Fenner
Jane C. Forster
Rosalie H. Franks
David Frolick
Mitchell Gerber
Jonathan Goldstein
Geoffrey Giles
Matthew A. Girson
Charlene Gould
Oliver Griffin
Johnpeter Horst Grill
David Hackett
Thomas Hegarty
John-Paul Himka
Keith Holtz
Paul Jaskot
Larry Jones
Milton Katz
Irving Kelter
Katharine Kennedy
Sally Kent
Jeffrey Kleiman
Norman Kravitz
S. Lillian Kremer
Robert Kunath
Andreas Hermann Kunze
Debbie Lackerstein
Mary Lagerway
Uta Larkey
Marshall Lee
Russel Lemmons
Gerald Lenthall
Raymond Leonard

Stuart Liebman
Kevin Madigan
Fred Marquardt
Wendell Mauter
Barbara McCloskey
Jeff McEwen
Jeffrey McIllwain
David Meier
Judith M. Melton
Julie Mewhort Klein
Paul Miller
Bob Moore
David Murphy
Helene Myers
Judith Nysenholc
William Oldson
Eliz Oljar
Leonard Orr
Steven T. Ostovich
Tony Paddock
Douglas Peifer
Elizabeth Peifer
Keith Pickus
Igor Pistry
Alexis E. Pogorelskin
Nadezhda K. Radina
Lynn Rapaport
Barrie Ratcliffe
Rondall Rice
Daniel Rogers
Katherine L. Rohrer
Barry Rothaus
Michael Rothberg
Thomas Saylor
Carl Schaffer
Donald Schilling
Michael Schuldiner
Donald Schwartz
Roy Schwartzman
Jesse L. Scott
Edith Shaked
Paul Shankman

Sanford Silverberg
Amy R. Sims
Ronald Smelser
David Snyder
Kevin P. Spicer
Roderick Stackelberg
L. M. Stallbaumer
Tamas Stark
Lionel Steiman
John W. Steinberg
Anthony Steinhoff
Laurinda Stryker
Marvin Swartz
Pamela E. Swett
Charles S. Thomas

Donald Thomas
Larry Thompson
Andrea Tyndall
Paul Vincent
James Walker
James Waller
Joseph R. White
Jonathan Wiesen
Larry Wilcox
Paul J. Wilson
Larry Witherell
Lee T. Wyatt III
Eric Yonke
Anna Ziebinska-Witek
Hebert Ziegle

FELLOWS (GRADUATE STUDENTS) (1996–2002)

Naomi Azriele
David Barsness
Rachel Baum
David Brenner
Nancy Brown
Michael Bryant
Kristina Busse
Diedre Butler
Gregory Caplan
Catherine Chatterley
Jolene Chu
Katy Crossley
Eliot Dickinson
Robert Drake
Hilary Earl
Michelle Erickson
Lynne Fallwell
Ron Feldman
Susan Fleming
Shannon L. Fogg
Kari R. Foster
Dennis Friedler
Max Friedman
Mitsuhiro Fujimaki

Alexandra Garbarini
Daniel Gauvin
S. David Glunt
Rachel Greenwald
Nathan Godley
Rebecca L. Golberg
Barnet Harston
Maureen Healy
Richard Hitchens
Daniel Inkelas
Kyle Jantzen
Mark Jantzen
Michael Jones
Christine Kulke
Katerina Lagos
Jennifer Levi
David Levy
Brad Lucas
Wendy A. Maier
Linda Maizels
Bruce McCord
Steven McCullough
Mark A. Mengerink
Dirk Moses

Lisa Moses
Jessica Nash
Ranen Omer
Andrew Oppengheimer
Katrin Paehler
Ellen L. Paul
Thomas Pegelow
Aimee L. Pozorski
Alexander Prussin
David Rolfs
Pamela M. Salela
Carol Scherer
Brian Schiff
Thilo Wolfgang Schimmel
Albert Schmidt
Paul Schweitzer
Carla Shapiro

Yael Simon
Lisa Skitol
Deborah Staines
Fran Sterling
Shane Stufflet
Mark Ellis Swartzburg
Jason Tavares
Melissa Jane Taylor
Martin Vann
Gregory Weeks
Gary Weissman
Laurie Anne Whitcomb
Robert Willingham
Rebecca Wittmann
Jamie Wraight
Anna Ziebinska-Witek
Jeffrey T. Zalar

Bibliography

Browning, Christopher. "A Product of Euphoria in Victory." Pp. 39–49 in *The Holocaust*, ed. D. Niewyck. Boston: Houghton Mifflin, 1997.

———. *Ordinary Men: Reserve Police Battalion 101 and the Final Solution in Poland.* New York: HarperCollins, 1998.

Flanzbaum, Helene, ed. *The Americanization of the Holocaust.* Baltimore: Johns Hopkins University Press, 1999.

Fleming, Gerald. "It Is the Fuhrer's Wish." Pp. 12–26 in *The Holocaust*, ed. D. Niewyk. Boston: Houghton Mifflin, 1997.

Goldhagen, Daniel Jonah. *Hitler's Willing Executioners, Ordinary Germans, and the Holocaust.* New York: Vintage Books, 1997.

Hayes, Peter, ed. *Lessons and Legacies: The Meaning of the Holocaust in a Changing World.* Evanston, Ill.: Northwestern University Press, 1991.

———. *Lessons and Legacies: Volume 3. Memory, Memorialization, and Denial.* Evanston, Ill.: Northwestern University Press, 1999.

Herzog, Dagmar. *Intimacy and Exclusion: Religious Politics in Pre-Revolutionary Baden.* Princeton, N. J.: Princeton University Press, 1996.

Hilberg, Raul. *The Destruction of the European Jews.* New York: Holmes and Meier, 1985.

———. *The Politics of Memory: The Journey of a Holocaust Historian.* Chicago: Ivan R. Dee, 1996.

Levi, Primo. *The Reawakening.* New York: Macmillan, 1965.

Marrus, Michael. *The Holocaust in History.* New York: Meridian, 1987.

Mommsen, Hans. "There Was No Fuhrer Order." Pp. 27–38 in *The Holocaust*, ed. D. Niewyk. Boston: Houghton Mifflin, 1997.

Niewyk, Donald L., ed. *The Holocaust* (2nd ed.). Boston: Houghton Mifflin, 1997.

Novick, Peter. *The Holocaust in American Life.* Boston: Houghton Mifflin, 1999.

Reddel, Carl, series ed. *Forging the Sword.* Vol. 5. Military History Symposium Series, United States Air Force Academy. Chicago: Imprint Publications, 1998.

Rosenfeld, Alvin H., ed. *Thinking about the Holocaust after Half a Century.*
Bloomington: Indiana University Press, 1997.

Schilling, Donald G., ed. *Lessons and Legacies: Vol. 2. Teaching the Holocaust
in a Changing World.* Evanston, Ill.: Northwestern University Press,
1998.

Spitzer, Leo. *Hotel Bolivia: Memories of a Refuge from Nazism.* New York:
Hill and Weng, 1998.

Wiesel, Elie. *Night.* New York: Bantam Books, 1960.

Yahil, Leni. *The Holocaust: The Fate of European Jewry, 1932–1945.* New
York: Oxford University Press, 1990.

About the Author

Anita Weiner, Ph.D., has been a faculty member of the Haifa University School of Social Work since 1969. As an institutional historian, she has published books on the history of childrens' institutions in Israel and on the contribution of the American Jewish Joint Distribution Committee to the renewal of Jewish life in the former Soviet Union. She lives in Haifa, Israel, with her husband, two sons, and seven grandchildren.